IMPROVING
NURSERY DEPARTMENTS

This Book
presented to the

CHURCH
LIBRARY
by

Dorothy Neal

Code 436-371, No. 1, Broadman Supplies, Nashville, Tenn. Printed in USA

Improving
Nursery Departments

POLLY HARGIS DILLARD

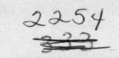
CONVENTION PRESS

Nashville, Tennessee

© 1959 · CONVENTION PRESS
Nashville, Tennessee

511-01723

Reprinted 1960

Code Number: Church Study Course for Teaching and Training

This book is number 1723 in category 17 or 1823 in category 18, section A

Library of Congress Catalog Card Number: 59-14429

Printed in the United States of America
7.5 AL 60 R.R.D.

About the Author

POLLY HARGIS DILLARD writes out of a wealth of experience in working with children, teaching workers with children, and writing for and about children.

Following her graduation from the University of Kentucky, her native state, she served in the Department of Elementary Sunday School Work of the Baptist Sunday School Board while completing requirements for the M.A. degree in elementary education at George Peabody College in Nashville. Subsequently, she served for seven years as superintendent of Beginner work in the Sunday School Department of the Baptist Sunday School Board.

For four years she was director of children's work and kindergarten teacher at the Main Street Baptist Church, Hattiesburg, Mississippi. From this position she went to the faculty of the School of Religious Education at the Southern Baptist Theological Seminary, Louisville, Kentucky, in 1953. While teaching children's work at the Seminary and serving as the director of the school's Nursery School and Kindergarten, she was at various times director of children's work for Deer Park Baptist Church and Highland Baptist Church, where she is now superintendent of a Beginner department in Sunday school and a worker in the Three-Year department of the Training Union.

Her writings include articles in denominational periodicals and curriculum materials for Nursery and Beginner workers, in addition to the following books: *Teaching the Beginner Child* (1948), *Sunday with Stevie* (1956), *Peter and the Rain* (1957), and *The Church Kindergarten* (1958).

Mrs. Dillard is married to Badgett Dillard, manager of administrative services for the Southern Baptist Theological Seminary.

Church Study Course for Teaching and Training

THE CHURCH STUDY COURSE for Teaching and Training began October 1, 1959. It is a merger of three courses previously promoted by the Sunday School Board—the Sunday School Training Course, the Graded Training Union Study Course, and the Church Music Training Course.

The course is fully graded. The system of awards provides a series of five diplomas of twenty books each for Adults or Young People, one diploma of ten books for Young People, two diplomas of five books each for Intermediates, and two diplomas of five books each for Juniors. Book awards earned previously in the Sunday School Training Course, the Graded Training Union Study Course, and the Church Music Training Course may be transferred to the new course.

The course is comprehensive, with books grouped into nineteen categories. The purpose of the course is to (1) help Christians to grow in knowledge and conviction; (2) help them grow toward maturity in Christian character and competence for service; (3) encourage them to participate worthily as workers in their churches; and (4) develop leaders for all phases of church life and work.

The Church Study Course for Teaching and Training is promoted by the Baptist Sunday School Board, 127 Ninth Avenue, North, Nashville, Tennessee, through its Sunday School, Training Union, Church Music, and Church Administration departments, and by these same departments in the states affiliated with the Southern Baptist Convention. A complete description of the course and the system of awards may be found in the *Church Study Course for Teaching and Training* catalog which may be obtained without charge from any one of these departments.

A record of all awards earned should be maintained in each church. A person should be designated by the church to keep the files. Forms for such records may be ordered from any Baptist Book Store.

Requirements for Credit in Class
or Home Study

IF CREDIT IS DESIRED for the study of this book in a class or by home study, the following requirements must be met:

I. IN CLASSWORK

1. The class must meet a minimum of seven and one-half clock hours. The required time does not include assembly periods. Ten class periods of forty-five minutes each are recommended. (If laboratory or clinical work is desired in specialized or technical courses, this requirement may be met by six clock hours of classwork and three clock hours of supervised laboratory or clinical work.)

2. A class member who attends all class sessions and completes the reading of the book within a week following the last class session will not be required to do any written work.

3. A class member who is absent from one or more sessions must answer the questions (pp. 144-145) on all chapters he misses. In such a case, he must turn in his paper within a week, and he must certify that he has read the book.

4. The teacher should request an award for himself. A person who teaches a book in section B, C, or D of any category or conducts an approved unit of instruction for Nursery, Beginner, or Primary children will be granted an award in category 11, Special Studies, which will count as an elective on his own diploma. He should specify in his request the name of the book taught, or the unit conducted for Nursery, Beginner, or Primary children.

5. The teacher should complete the Request for Book Awards—Class Study (Form 150) and forward it within two weeks after the completion of the class to the Church Study Course Awards Office, 127 Ninth Avenue, North, Nashville 3, Tennessee.

II. IN HOME STUDY

1. A person who does not attend any class session may receive credit by answering all questions for written work as indicated

in the book (pp. 144-145). When a person turns in his paper on home study, he must certify that he has read the book.

2. Students may find profit in studying the text together, but individual papers are required. Carbon copies or duplicates in any form cannot be accepted.

3. Home study work papers may be graded by the pastor or a person designated by him, or they may be sent to the Church Study Course Awards Office for grading. The form entitled Request for Book Awards—Home Study (Form 151) must be used in requesting awards. It should be mailed to Church Study Course Awards Office, 127 Ninth Avenue, North, Nashville 3, Tennessee.

III. CREDIT FOR THIS BOOK

A person may earn credit for this book in either category 17 (No. 1723) or category 18 (No. 1823), section A.

Class Study—Separate copies of Form 150, Request for Book Awards—Class Study, must be used for each category when making requests.

Home Study—The category in which credit is desired must be indicated on Form 151—Request for Book Awards—Home Study, when requesting credit for home study of this book.

Contents

Some Audio-Visual Materials

For Use in Teaching This Book

THE FOLLOWING LIST of audio-visual materials will be helpful in teaching this book. In some instances more materials are listed than it would be practical to use. In such cases, select the frames of the filmstrips and portions of motion pictures that contribute more directly to the particular chapter of the book you are teaching and that more nearly meet the needs of the group you are teaching.

FILMSTRIPS

Guiding Nursery Children
Providing for Nursery Children
Sources of Truth, Part 1 (Know Your Child Series)
The Dynamics of Growth, Part 2 (Know Your Child Series)
First Steps in Religion

MOTION PICTURES

Life with Baby
The Terrible Two's and the Trusting Three's

CHAPTER 1

I. IMPORTANCE OF NURSERY WORKERS

II. CHARACTERISTICS OF NURSERY WORKERS

1. See the World Through the Eyes of the Nursery Child
2. Inspire Confidence and Security
3. Accept Children as They Are
4. Recognize Differences
5. Are Sensitive to Needs
6. Are Christlike in Daily Living
7. Are Bible Students
8. Are Mature Christians

III. WAYS OF BECOMING A BETTER WORKER

1. Prescription for Growth
2. Self-checking
3. Some Do's for Nursery Workers

IV. DISTRIBUTION OF RESPONSIBILITY

1. Superintendent or Leader
2. Associates
3. Co-ordinator
4. Secretary
5. The Director of Children's Work

V. NURSERY CORRELATING COMMITTEE

1. Organization
2. Responsibility

VI. THE EXTENDED SESSION

1

Facing the Challenge

A CHILD is constantly storing up feelings, reactions, and impressions that become the groundwork for his personality, character, and later behavior. This development does not just happen. A child learns first from those who are near to him and whom he loves—his parents. As his world enlarges to include workers at church, he learns from them. A worker's faith in and attitude toward God, her relationship with other people, and her adjustment to life are all reflected in her guidance of the child. She tells the child how she feels about the Bible by the way she handles it and by her tone of voice as she reads it. Her attitude toward "our church" affects greatly the attitude of the child. She teaches by everything she does, even by casual words and acts when she may not be conscious of their influence.

I. IMPORTANCE OF NURSERY WORKERS

The most important factor in the teaching of Nursery children is the worker—more important than equipment, space, materials, activities, stories, or songs. Attitudes, ideas, and feelings go out from you to the child with whom you associate, and he in turn responds to you.

II. CHARACTERISTICS OF NURSERY WORKERS

YOU, the Nursery worker, are guiding the changes that take place in the way a child feels, thinks, and acts. What are some of the characteristics which Nursery workers should seek to develop?

1

1. *See the World Through the Eyes of the Nursery Child*

How difficult it must be to be a toddler, a two-year-old, or a three-year-old, and live in a world planned for adults. Nothing fits the small size of the Nursery child. The furniture is for grownups. A child must wait for the convenience of grownups for many things. To the Nursery child the world seems to have been planned for giants. One little boy complained as he walked down the street, "All I can see is feet, feet, feet."

Adults have had so many things to learn that, in many cases, they have forgotten how a child sees, feels, thinks, and the way he interprets everyday experiences. The Nursery child needs workers who have the ability to see as he sees, to think as he thinks, and to feel as he feels.

2. *Inspire Confidence and Security*

Children need workers who are sympathetic, friendly, happy, and loving. The child who finds workers like this in his church room thinks of the church as a happy place and feels secure when Mother or Daddy leaves him at the door of his department.

3. *Accept Children as They Are*

Children need workers who accept them as they are— Mary with her thumb-sucking, Bill with his temper tantrums, and Susan with her bossiness. Workers accept the child as he is and see him as he can become. They accept his feelings and try to understand them. They help a child to understand that they know how he feels, and that sometimes they feel this way, too.

4. *Recognize Differences*

Children need workers who recognize that each child is different, that each child has his own rate of growth and should not be compared with others. Each child's reaction to a situation is different from every other child's reaction. His experiences consist, not of the situations, but of his reaction to them.

5. Are Sensitive to Needs

Children need workers who recognize and are sensitive to the basic needs of the developing personality—the need to know, to belong, to love and be loved, and to feel secure. Other needs grow out of these. To meet these needs a worker must know each individual child.

6. Are Christlike in Daily Living

Children need workers who acknowledge the lordship of Christ and follow him daily. Some people profess to know Christ, but fail to obey him in all areas of life. They can quote accurately, "Thou shalt love the Lord thy God . . . , and thy neighbour as thyself" (Luke 10:27), but when it comes to the test of loving everyone, they fail.

Jesus did not just tell people about God. He revealed God through his daily contacts with people as he worked with them, ate with them, and lived with them. Words mean very little to children. They need to see examples.

7. Are Bible Students

Children need workers who are students of the Bible. The better the worker understands the Bible, the better he or she can interpret it to the children. The greater the knowledge of the Bible, the deeper will be one's appreciation and love for it. Workers with Nursery children should know what they believe about God, Jesus, the Bible, and the church, and why they believe it.

8. Are Mature Christians

Children need workers who are spiritually mature, workers

who are loving, forgiving, trusting, and who extend their warmth and concern to all people.

III. Ways of Becoming a Better Worker

Every worker with Nursery children can and should become the kind of worker which children need. You can become that worker if you will.

1. *Prescription for Growth*

(1) Seek to grow in your own Christian life through Bible study, prayer, and Christian service.

A worker with three-year-olds once said, "I'd like to work in the Young People's department. There I will have to study my Bible." What this worker did not realize is that she should have been studying her Bible all along. The more a worker studies the Bible, the better she can interpret the Bible to the Nursery child.

(2) Study each individual child. Each child is a distinct personality, with individual needs, interests, experiences, and abilities. He must be taught as an individual. There is no such thing as mass teaching for children. What is good for one may not be good for another.

(3) Learn how to use more effectively materials which are suitable for Nursery children.

(4) Observe other people at work with children. Good nursery schools offer an opportunity for such learning.

(5) Look at yourself. Understand yourself. Most people find it hard to understand themselves. They do not know why they do and say things which they never intended to do and say.

2. *Self-checking*

Are you the kind of worker Nursery children need? Find out by asking yourself these questions. Check "yes" or "no" to each of them.

	Yes	No
1. Do I really like children?	____	____
2. Do I see the world as a child sees it?	____	____
3. Do I bring out the best in the children?	____	____
4. Am I a friend to children?	____	____
5. Do I use words which the children understand?	____	____
6. Do I let the children do as much as they are able to do for themselves?	____	____
7. Do I laugh with the children and not at them?	____	____
8. Do I treat children with as much consideration and respect as I do adults?	____	____
9. Do I see and understand each child as a growing person?	____	____
10. Do I appreciate and work well with parents?	____	____
11. Do I work well with fellow workers?	____	____
12. Am I sensitive to the needs of the children and to what they are feeling and thinking?	____	____
13. Do I give of myself in time, love, and service?	____	____
14. Do I make thorough preparation for each session?	____	____
15. Do I study the Bible daily? Do I try to live daily the principles which I find in the Bible?	____	____
16. Do I recognize that behind behavior there is a reason? Do I try to find the reason?	____	____
17. Am I eager to grow and learn more about children's interests, development, and guidance?	____	____

Your self-checking may result, at first, in discouragement. It will no doubt point up at least some areas in which you need improvement. Remember, we are considering ways you can become a better worker. The value of your self-checking lies in what you do about the matter after you measure yourself. Effective workers are always growing workers.

3. Some Do's for Nursery Workers

A Nursery worker will be guided in her actions by the specific situations with which she is confronted. However, there are certain practices which are basic to working effectively with small children.

1. Remove your hat.
2. Get down on the child's level, even if it means sitting on the floor most of the time.
3. Use a soft voice.
4. Listen and observe more than you talk.
5. Help each child to know how to use materials.
6. Avoid talking about children in their presence. Devote your time to listening to the children rather than to talking about them.
7. Use action with words. Help a child to put away blocks instead of saying, "Put the blocks on the shelf."
8. Commend the children when they accomplish something for themselves. Avoid "gushing."
9. Allow the child plenty of time to do something. Don't rush him, but be patient. And don't rush about the room yourself.
10. Be alert to see opportunities to enrich the child's experiences by singing, talking, or just listening.
11. Be in the room at least 30 minutes before the session.
12. Avoid moralizing, such as "God doesn't like that," or "Jesus isn't happy when you do that."
13. Offer a child a choice only if you intend to let him make the decision. Avoid "Would you like to go home?" unless he is to make the decision.
14. Avoid comparing children.
15. Use redirection (turning the child's attention to an act which has equal value to him).
16. Define limits clearly and maintain them consistently.
17. Encourage a child to talk freely about himself and his feelings toward others.
18. Be able to call by name the children with whom you work.

IV. DISTRIBUTION OF RESPONSIBILITY

Both men and women should be Nursery workers. Often men can meet special needs of children, and they like to have men in their department. It gives them a feeling of security. Men help to create a homelike situation.

Knowing his or her individual responsibility in a Nursery department helps a worker to be efficient. The upset, unsure worker causes the children to be upset and unsure.

In every Nursery room there should be at least two workers—a Sunday school superintendent or a Training Union leader, and an associate. The following ratio of workers to children is desirable:

Age Group	Enrolment	Superintendent or Leader	Associates
Babies	12	1	2
Toddlers	15	1	3
Two-year-olds	20	1	4
Three-year-olds	20	1	4

1. *Superintendent or Leader*

The full responsibility for all the procedure in the department rests on the superintendent or leader. Specifically, he or she will have the following responsibilities:

(1) Lead other workers in planning for each session, including the extended session.

(2) Help workers in learning more about working with children.

(3) Visit each enrolled child in the department.

(4) Work in co-operation with workers of the particular age group from other church organizations.

(5) Assume responsibility for parent meetings (a full discussion of this appears in chapter 8).

(6) Assume responsibility for cleanliness and care of room and equipment.

2. *Associates*

All those who work with the superintendent or leader are known as associates. The specific responsibilities of an associate include the following:

(1) *Visitation.*—Each quarter the associate visits the children assigned and takes *Living with Children* to the homes according to the schedule agreed upon. Other visits are made to win unsaved parents to Christ, to establish family worship, or to meet other needs.

(2) *Area of activity.*—Each associate is responsible for planning and preparing a definite area of activity. The worker has the major responsibility for guiding experiences in this area during a session. However there are some conditions which would call for a worker moving from the original area. Factors influencing such a movement are size of room, number of children, number of workers, number of activities, needs of the child, experience of the worker, or emergencies.

(3) *Planning meetings.*—Attendance at planning meetings is a must for every worker. Preparation for the next session, improvement of teaching ability, and spiritual growth for the worker are the results of good planning. Workers should faithfully support this phase of department work.

3. *Co-ordinator*

When a church has three or more Nursery departments, it is wise to elect co-ordinators. One co-ordinator may serve with the Sunday school, one with the Training Union, and another for weekday activities.

Some of the duties of the Nursery co-ordinator are to (1) assist in discovering, enlisting, and training Nursery workers; (2) work with the minister of education and Sunday school superintendent and/or Training Union director; (3) unify the work of the Nursery department (advise about transfers, parent meetings, planning meetings, and other phases of the work); (4) act as hostess and direct the coming and going of parents so that it is not necessary for parents to enter any of the Nursery rooms; (5) act as consultant regarding rooms and equipment; (6) share responsibility for the Nursery extended session; (7) serve on the Nursery correlating committee and assist in unifying the work with all children of Nursery age.

Because of the broad scope of the Nursery co-ordinator's duties, his other church responsibilities should be limited.

4. *Secretary*

There are no Nursery department secretaries. The superintendent or leader marks the record card. Each child is marked only on attendance. Each worker is marked on all points in the record system as used by the organization.

A general Nursery secretary handles the records for all the Nursery departments. The record is picked up at the department. When all of the records have been collected, the general Nursery secretary compiles the report and takes it to the general secretary. At the beginning of a session the secretary may serve as a hostess to help parents as they arrive. During the session, while not involved in handling records, the secretary may assist the co-ordinator in any way that may be needed.

5. *The Director of Children's Work*

Due to the rapidly expanding educational programs, many churches have found it wise to employ a director of children's work. This person serves in a supervisory position to the volunteer workers with children. Specific responsibilities in relation to Nursery departments are:

(1) Co-operate in enlisting and training workers.
(2) Lead each department to do its best work.
(3) Co-ordinate the work of all departments and organizations.

V. NURSERY CORRELATING COMMITTEE

This committee helps co-ordinate all of the work of the various church organizations as it relates to Nursery children.

The members are elected annually by the church at the same time other standing church committees are elected. The committee meets regularly once each quarter and more often as the need arises. Problems relating to any phase of Nursery work are referred to this committee.

1. *Organization*

If the church has a director of children's work, she may serve as chairman of the correlating committee. Otherwise, a person who is well informed on Nursery work may be the chairman. Other people on the committee are as follows: (1) one or more parents who act as parent representatives; (2) a deacon, preferably the father of a Nursery child; (3) Sunday school and Training Union Nursery co-ordinators and weekday co-ordinator; (4) Cradle Roll superintendent. (Where churches do not have co-ordinators, superintendents and leaders represent their organizations.) The pastor, Sunday school superintendent, Training Union director, minister of education, and minister of music may serve as ex officio members of the committee. The chart on page 15 shows the organization of a Nursery committee.

2. *Responsibility*

Some of the responsibilities of the committee are as follows: (1) Work out Nursery policies to be adopted by the church. (See booklet *Suggestions for Nursery Correlating Committee* for suggested policies.) (2) Help the entire church membership become aware of the Nursery policies. (3) Consider requests for Nursery equipment and supplies. The committee should make an evaluation of each request. If the supplies and equipment should be bought, the committee recommends their purchase to the church. (4) Strengthen parent-worker relationship. (5) Supervise cleanliness and care of the Nursery rooms and equipment. (6) Establish and give general oversight to the extended sessions.

VI. The Extended Session

An extended session is planned for the child whose parents attend the Sunday morning or Sunday night worship service. The session is important because it provides additional opportunities for teaching. The child remains in the room where he has been for the previous session. The program meets the needs of the individual child. The child uses materials and equipment with which he is familiar.

The extended session is not a "baby-sitting" time. It is important that at least one worker from the previous session be in the extended session. The worker knows the children and will know what has taken place during the previous session. Many children are upset by unfamiliar faces. The presence of a regular worker who has been in the Nursery department during the preceding Sunday school or Training Union period helps both the child and the parents feel more secure.

The extended session is of value to the worker. The time spent with the children enables the worker to know them better and to do a more effective job of teaching.

The workers in a Nursery department may rotate for the extended session. The schedule should be planned well in advance, thus enabling the worker to make any necessary arrangements. Parents may assist the regular worker in the extended session when needed. It usually is not wise to use the parent in the same room in which his child will be staying. Through their experiences in the extended session parents can be helped to understand the philosophy and methods of Nursery work and so to become better teachers with their own children.

A schedule should be posted where each worker can check it from time to time, and the superintendent or leader keeps a copy. The following is a sample of a schedule which may be worked out:

Department *Nursery 4* (*Three-year-olds*)
Extended Session for *January-March*

January	February	March
4	1	1
Teachers	*Teachers*	*Teachers*
Mrs. Smith	Mrs. Smith	Mrs. Smith
Mrs. Lane	Mrs. Jacob	Mr. Lee
11	8	8
Teachers	*Teachers*	*Teachers*
Miss Wood	Miss Wood	Miss Wood
Mr. Stiles	Mrs. Hollar	Miss Gray
18	15	15
Teachers	*Teachers*	*Teachers*
Mr. Jones	Mr. Jones	Mr. Jones
Mrs. Moody	Mrs. Kent	Mrs. Arnold
25	22	22
Teachers	*Teachers*	*Teachers*
Mrs. Seebold	Mrs. Seebold	Mrs. Seebold
Mr. Cook	Miss Dansby	Mr. Seebold
		29
		Teachers
		Mrs. Smith
		Mrs. Lee

Some churches follow the policy of using the same workers every thirteenth Sunday. This means, for example, that Mrs. Lane, who assisted in the extended session January 4, will help again on April 5, June 28, and September 27. Some workers prefer each Sunday for an entire month. Then there are several months in which the worker does not participate in the extended session. Those who are to assist in the extended session receive copies of *Church Nursery Guide* and attend the planning meeting.

Workers need to know before the extended session which children are staying. A chart similar to the one shown may be conveniently placed for parents to check their child's name. Knowing which children are remaining enables the worker to prevent a child from being unhappy when his parent does not come for him.

Extended Session   Date: May 21
Teachers: Mrs. Lee
          Miss Wood
My child is staying for the extended session
          (Parents list names of children who are staying.)

The children are taken to the bathroom, one or two at a time, for toileting and washing hands. One cup of fruit juice, milk, or water, and one cracker are served. This should be a snack, not a meal. Two-year-olds and three-year-olds help serve the drink and crackers. Children will enjoy using colored cups and napkins. The worker thanks God for the fruit juice and crackers, or leads the children to thank God.

By this time the children will need to rest. Mats or cots are placed in the room for the children to lie on when they finish their juice. Soft music on the record player helps to make a desirable transition from juice to rest. If a record player is not available, a worker may hum or softly sing lullabies or hymns. Sometimes gently rubbing a child's back or sitting near him will help a restless child to relax. If workers lie down, it often helps the children relax. One worker should remain seated in order to observe the entire room and move easily to any point. Any movement in the room is a distraction. The length of time for resting will depend upon the need of the children. Sometimes ten minutes is sufficient. At other times the children may need twenty minutes or more. If any children go to sleep, do not disturb them.

After resting, the children may use the same materials which they have used previously. If the worker feels that it is wise, new activities such as soap painting or finger painting may be used.

Before the time for parents to arrive, the worker and the children begin to put away materials. Time should be allowed for doing this without hurrying the children in their efforts to participate.

In determining the schedules for the extended session, certain important factors must be considered: number of children, needs, interest, equipment, and space. Adjustments must be made to meet the needs of each local situation.

SUGGESTED ACTIVITIES

For Workers Who Study This Book

1. Recall some of the people whom you consider to be good workers with children.
   (1) List the qualities which they have that made an impression on you.
   (2) Compare their qualities with those suggested in this chapter.
   (3) List the qualities which you are going to strive for in the future.
2. In one column list the things which you do as a Nursery worker. In a parallel column list the things which you should be doing. Compare the two columns to determine how you can make your work more effective.

ORGANIZATION OF THE NURSERY COMMITTEE

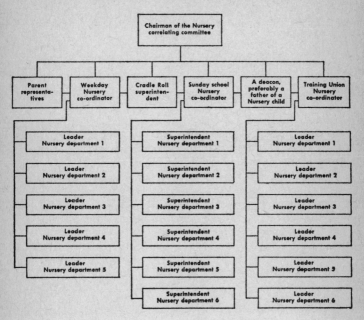

From *The Sunday School Builder,* October, 1958

CHAPTER 2

I. GOD'S PLAN FOR INDIVIDUAL GROWTH
    1. According to Pattern
    2. Avenues of Learning

II. CHARACTERISTICS OF EACH AGE GROUP

III. INFORMATION NEEDED ON EACH CHILD

IV. WAYS OF KNOWING A CHILD
    1. Through Questionnaires
    2. By Visitation
    3. By Casual Contact
    4. By Observation in Nursery School
    5. Through Information from Other Workers
    6. By Studying Books on Child Development

2

Studying the Nursery Child

GOD HAS A PLAN for growth. This is evident in the fact that human beings must pass through a long learning period before they become adults. This period is a part of God's plan for people whom he has made and equipped to think and to work for him.

I. GOD'S PLAN FOR INDIVIDUAL GROWTH

"Jesus increased in wisdom and stature, and in favour with God and man" (Luke 2:52). Jesus followed God's plan for growth. God's plan is not casual nor haphazard; it is organized and orderly.

God's plan is for mental, physical, social, emotional, and spiritual growth to be interwoven. Each is dependent upon the other. For example, a child's spiritual growth is dependent upon his mental, physical, social, and emotional development. A daddy leaves his three-year-old at the door of her department and hurries away without giving her a chance to tell him good-by. She feels alone and unhappy. All morning she mopes in a corner and refuses to participate in any of the activities. This three-year-old's association with the church is an unhappy one.

1. *According to Pattern*

Each change in growth depends upon what has preceded it and affects what comes after it. A baby can throw his toy on the floor, can lean over and see it, and can want it again before he has the physical ability to get it back. Certain

17

developments in muscle co-ordination must take place before the baby can pick up the toy.

Each child follows the same general pattern of growth, but each child's rate of growth is different. One child may walk at the age of twelve months, another not until the age of fifteen months. This fact does not mean that the child who was slower in walking is not normal. It only means that one child has a slower rate of muscular development than the other child. This is true in all phases of growth.

2. Avenues of Learning

God has planned that each child learn through certain avenues.

(1) *Through the senses.*—Probably the earliest to develop and the most basic avenues of learning are the sensory perceptions: touching, hearing, seeing, tasting, smelling. The two-year-old, touching the soft velvety petals of the flower and smelling its fragrance as a worker tells about God's making the flowers, is using seeing, hearing, smelling, and touching to learn about the wonders of God. The baby hearing a worker's joyful tone of voice saying the word "Jesus," seeing the smile on the worker's face, and feeling the worker's love, is getting first impressions of Jesus.

(2) *Through curiosity.*—A child wants to know, to experiment, and to try. This desire leads him to ask questions, to explore the world around him, and to have an interest in things.

(3) *By doing.*—Doing for the Nursery child is in the form of play. This is serious business to him. In play, children begin to respond to each other and to learn the first steps in social living. They begin to learn to give and take and to share their toys because it is satisfying to do so. In play children begin to form desirable habits of thought, feeling, and action.

(4) *By imitation.*—A child copies what he sees others do,

whether good or bad. Attitudes, action, tones of voices, and language are all imitated by a child.

(5) *Through imagination.*—A three-year-old becomes the story child as he listens to a story, or "Daddy" as he plays out daddy experiences. Vicariously he has experiences through his imagination.

II. CHARACTERISTICS OF EACH AGE GROUP

In planning for teaching, selecting equipment and materials, choosing music and stories, Nursery workers must first answer such questions as: What is the child like at this age? What can he do? What are his special interests? What experiences has he had? For what experiences is he ready? What materials or experiences will stimulate his growth in each area—physically, mentally, socially, emotionally, and spiritually?

Although each child is a distinct individual, developing at his own rate, certain characteristics are common to each age group and significant for the workers.

As you study the characteristics of the baby, note how these characteristics are significant for the worker. Note also the many learning experiences a baby can have.

BABY

Characteristics	Significance for Workers
1. Likes the familiar	1. The room arrangement should give a feeling of familiarity. Mother may bring a familiar toy for play.
2. At times is shy	2. Allow only regular Nursery workers in the room. Strangers and others should remain outside.
3. Each one is different and has different needs	3. Keep the schedule card on the bed for use any time the child is brought to church.

4. Responds to music

4. Workers may sing to him and play records.

5. Constantly learning through his senses—tasting, smelling, hearing, seeing, and feeling

5. Workers should use soft voices and provide pleasant surroundings.

6. A social being

6. Enjoys playing such games as "peek-a-boo" with a worker; responds to worker by cooing, making other sounds.

7. Has own rate of growth

7. Workers recognize that each child has own rate of growth and do not compare one child with another. One child may walk or talk before another.

8. Easily upset

8. Provide a quiet environment, with secure Christian workers caring for the baby's needs.

In the following pictures note specific characteristics of the baby, and seek to discover how the workers are responding to these characteristics.

Likes the Familiar

At Times Is Shy

Each Has Different Needs

Responds to Music

A Social Person

Easily Upset

Workers with toddlers need to be aware of the child's increasing maturity and alert to see when he is ready for some new learning. On the other hand, they need to be understanding when he reverts to baby characteristics.

TODDLER

Characteristics	Significance for Workers
1. Active—moving continually from one thing to another	1. Provide plenty of space in which to move, and plenty of suitable materials.
2. Can do some things for himself	2. Allow him to do as much for himself as he can, such as enjoying toys without adult intervention, getting toys with which to play, and helping to put away toys.
3. Full of curiosity	3. Provide a place in which he can explore, touch, feel, and mouth everything within his reach.
4. Shows better co-ordination in use of fingers	4. Provide materials with which he can do these things—pull, lift, drag, push, dump, pour.
5. Likes to be near other children, but does not know how to play with them	5. Realize that a child will explore a person just like he does things, such as pushing or pulling another child.
6. Has short attention span	6. Worker does not interfere with activities, but supplies something else for child to do when he tires of an activity.
7. Beginning to form words	7. Worker uses familiar words with the child.

8. Sharing toys and taking turns are beyond him—holds what he has close to him and carries it around

8. Worker does not take toy unless it is absolutely necessary, and then offers an acceptable exchange so the child is not left empty-handed.

9. Adjustment is difficult

9. Room should be arranged in a similar way each time the child comes to church.

10. Part baby and part child—is taking many steps in growing up

10. Needs workers who will love him, have fun with him, and patiently teach him as he seems ready to learn without forcing him out of his ways of babyhood too quickly.

11. Beginning to learn that he is a person, capable of saying both "yes" and "no"

11. Workers accept his saying no as a part of his growing up process.

In the pictures which follow, note evidences of the toddler's growing independence.

Needs Space

Can Do Things for Himself

Full of Curiosity

Loves to Pull Things

Plays Alone

Plays with Worker

Uses Familiar Words

Sharing Is Beyond Him

Familiar Objects Aid Adjustment

Capable of Saying Yes and No

Development is often rapid from the toddler stage to the two-year-old. Note the growth evidenced in the following chart and pictures. Note, also, the limitations which are indicated. Workers must not expect a two-year-old to function like a three-year-old.

TWO-YEAR-OLD

Characteristics	Significance for Workers
1. Still very active—constantly on the move	1. Provide space for movement and challenge.
2. Likes to explore	2. Provide such materials as blocks, books, puzzles, and paints with which to work.
3. Likes to touch, to feel, to pat, and to pound materials	3. Provide materials such as clay for child to pat and pound.
4. Play is individual (parallel)	4. Provide more than one doll, puzzle or such materials, which may be used by more than one child at a time.
5. Short attention span	5. Provide a variety of materials to allow for short attention span and need to explore new worlds.
6. Beginning to enjoy short stories	6. Use short stories, usually about a picture. Tell same story again and again. Child wants stories about himself in relation to mother, daddy, and others.
7. Not ready for a group time	7. Do not have a group time.
8. Often not sociable	8. Worker accepts the fact that even though the child likes to have other children around and enjoys watching them play, his group participation is still very limited.

9. Play is simple

9. Provide materials suited to his interest, such as dolls, blocks, and puzzles.

10. Wants to know about everything

10. Worker willingly answers the child's questions and provides opportunities to discover things about himself. Be careful not to go beyond the child's understanding.

11. Begins to associate God with the wonders about him

11. Worker watches for opportunities in which to help the child become more aware of the wonders about him.

12. Can talk to God in his own way

12. Worker watches for opportunities to talk to God and to let the child talk to God. These are fleeting and may come after a child has looked at a picture, listened to a song, or smelled the flowers.

13. Can sing simple songs

13. Worker sings or hums songs with few words, simple melody, and experiences familiar to the child.

Very Active

Likes to Explore

Likes to Pat and Pound

Parallel Play

Enjoys Short Stories

Not a Social Person

Play Is Simple

Wants to Know About Everything

Begins to Associate God with
Wonders Around Him

Can Sing Simple Praise Songs

The charts and pictures we have been studying point up the rapid development of a child during the first three years of his life. Note the many ways in which three's are ahead of two's.

THREE-YEAR-OLD

Characteristics	Significance for Workers
1. Is active	1. Provide plenty of space, suitable equipment. Allow choices of activity and freedom to move from one activity to another.
2. Has short attention span	2. Provide a variety of activities. Use suitable stories, songs, and Bible verses properly adapted to the activities.
3. Forgets quickly	3. When necessary, remind the child of ways to use materials and better ways of doing things.
4. Is literal-minded	4. Use words the child understands. Symbolism such as "the lost sheep," "Jesus in your heart," "black heart," or "climbing up sunshine mountain" should be avoided.
5. Asks many questions	5. Answer questions in terms the child understands, giving only helpful information.
6. Learns through senses	6. Provide materials that stimulate and challenge a child to see, feel, smell, and investigate.
7. Can do many things for himself	7. Provide equipment which helps a child to do for himself (low rack for wraps); give child responsibilities within his range of ability.

8. Is imitative	8. Set a good example in using soft voices, being helpful, kind, thoughtful, and courteous.
9. Has vivid imagination	9. Provide such materials as paints, home-living, blocks, which will enable child to learn through imagination.
10. Has some ability to reason	10. Let child solve problems as well as he can before giving guidance.
11. Recognizes that the Bible is different from other books	11. Child has access to Bible (Bible 1450BP preferred) at all times.
12. Beginning to understand that Jesus loves him	12. Workers use stories and songs about Jesus which are adapted so the child can understand them.
13. Beginning to put into everyday living qualities of helpfulness, kindness, and thoughtfulness	13. Workers help parents become acquainted with what is being done at church. Seek to strengthen ties between church and home.

Allow Choice of Activity   **Short Attention Span**

Forgets Quickly

Literal-minded

Learns Through Senses

Growing in Independence

Is Imitative

Has Vivid Imagination

Some Ability to Reason

Recognizes Bible as a Different
Book

III. Information Needed on Each Child

Workers must know each individual child if they are to be the best teachers. It is not enough to know the characteristics of toddlers or two's or three's in general. The worker must know how each child is like the average for his age and how he varies from it. Deviation is normal. It is a mere truism to say that "the average child does not exist."

Workers must be aware of the need to know each child not only as they see him in the Nursery room, but also in every area of his living. They must cultivate a desire to know each child and an ability to note and interpret subtle indications of his interests and needs.

Some of the obvious things which workers need to discover about each child are—

1. FAMILY BACKGROUND: occupation of parents; church affiliation of parents; attitude of parents toward child; attitude of parents toward church; attitude of parents toward community; members of family; names and ages of children; type of discipline used with child; issues of disagreement between child and parents; daily routine followed in the home

2. SOCIAL ACTIVITIES: playmates; nursery school; church attendance; movie attendance; special groups; travel experience; reaction to other children; reaction to adults

3. SPECIAL INTERESTS: favorite play activities; favorite books, stories, toys; favorite radio and TV programs

4. HEALTH: serious illnesses or accidents; present health

5. PROBLEMS: physical and emotional

IV. Ways of Knowing a Child

Alert workers will be constantly aware of opportunities to know each child. Some planned ways to know him are listed. However, it must be remembered that the key to knowing a child rests on genuine love for him and on respect for him as a person.

1. *Through Questionnaires*

The questionnaire is one way in which an associate can obtain information on a child. It may be mailed or taken to each home. If it is mailed, an accompanying letter should explain the reason for the questionnaire. The letter may read something like this:

> *Dear Mrs. Smith:*
> *I am delighted that Paul is being transferred to our Nursery department. To help me be a "good" teacher this year, please fill out the enclosed questionnaire. This will help me to know Paul better.*
> *I will call you Tuesday to learn what will be a convenient time for me to pick up the questionnaire and talk with you.*
>
> > *Cordially,*
> > *Mary Jones*

If the associate takes the questionnaire to the home, she should explain it to the parent and leave it. A convenient time is set (with the parent) to pick up the questionnaire.

It is wise to have the questionnaire filled out and in the hands of the workers a month before a child is transferred. Sharing information at planning meetings helps workers to know each child in the Nursery department. This sharing is most important, since all the workers will work with all the children in the room.

The following questionnaire may be filled out by parents to help the worker know their child. The questionnaire for a specified Nursery age would contain the general information plus the specific information appropriate to that age.

GENERAL INFORMATION

Name ....Name Used.......

Address ....Tel. No. ....

Birthday: Month ....Day ....Year ....

Parents' names ....

Father's occupation ....

Mother's occupation (outside home) ....

If mother works, who keeps child? ....

Mother a Christian? ....Father a Christian? ....

Mother member of church? ....Where? ....

Father member of church? ....Where? ....

Where parents are during:

   Sunday school ....

   Training Union ....

   Other times ....

Other people living in the home...................................

....

Is child adopted? ....How old was child when adopted? ....

Serious illnesses or accidents....................................

....

Nature of handicaps, if any......................................

....

In addition to the foregoing information, a questionnaire for a baby would include the following:

Time child sleeps ....

Position of sleep: On stomach .... On back ....

Other ....

Position for feeding: Held in arms ....

Placed in bed with bottle .... Other ....

....

Food: Milk .... Time ....

Juice .... Time .... Other ....

Time .... Any allergies ....

What? ....

Bubbling: During feeding .... After feeding ....

Other .... Shots: Kind ....

Date .... Kind .... Date ....

Kind .... Date ....

(Above to be filled by parents as child received his shots)

Comments: (changes in schedule or special instructions) ....
....
....

A questionnaire for a toddler would add the following to the general questions. Workers may wish to include some of the items on the list for babies.

Words child uses for daily needs, such as going to the bathroom, etc.
....

If child does not use words, how does he make his needs known?.....
....

Schedule followed: (sleeping) ....

(eating) ....

Past problems: Illnesses ....

Fears ....

Discipline ....

For two- and three-year-olds, the questionnaire, in addition to the items of general information, and perhaps some on the toddler's list, would include the following.

Any pets? ....

Favorite toy .... Experiences outside the home ......,..

Ways of discipline ....

Any problems (thumb-sucking, nail-biting, fears) ....
....

The questionnaire should be placed in a notebook where workers can study it from time to time. Place on a card the brief information needed regularly about the baby. This card may be placed on the bed or nearby.

2. By Visitation

The person who knows a child best is the mother. Even though a parent has filled out a questionnaire, a friendly visit to the home can reveal more about a child than the questions answered by the parents. Hopes and ambitions for their child, things about which they worry concerning him, and many experiences will be revealed in a visit.

3. By Casual Contact

Casual contacts with the parents and child in the grocery store, department store, or other places will help an alert worker to understand a child better.

4. By Observation in Nursery School

Observing a child in the nursery school or child care center which he attends will bring to light any problems which the child may have. Workers can observe how these problems are handled by those who are with the child each day.

5. Through Information from Other Workers

Those who have worked with the child previously in the church can pass on to present workers valuable information about the child. Past experiences play an important part in the way a child learns. Workers need to know these experiences.

6. By Studying Books on Child Development

There are many books and publications in the field of child development. A study of these will help a worker to increase her knowledge about children in general and enable her to solve some of the behavior problems which arise. See chapter 9 for suggested list.

SUGGESTED ACTIVITIES

For Workers Who Study This Book

1. Select a child from the age group with which you work.
   (1) Use the questionnaire in this chapter to write down all you know about the child.
   (2) Make definite plans for getting to know the child better.
2. Select another child from the same age group.
   (1) Compare his behavior with that which is common to his present level of development and is accepted as such.
   (2) Write down the behavior which is not common to this stage of development. What do you think is causing his deviation in behavior?

CHAPTER 3

I. PROVIDING DESIRABLE ROOMS

    1. Space
    2. Location
    3. Floor Coverings
    4. Lighting
    5. Heating
    6. Walls
    7. Supply Cabinets
    8. Toilet Facilities
    9. Reception Areas
   10. Kitchenette
   11. Provision for Wraps
   12. Some Don't's in Planning for Nursery Children

II. PLANNING FOR AGE GROUPING

    1. Four or Five Rooms
    2. Three Rooms
    3. Two Rooms
    4. One Room

III. PRINCIPLES OF ROOM ARRANGEMENT

IV. SUGGESTED ROOM ARRANGEMENTS

3

Providing Room for Growth

NURSERY ROOMS should help children to grow—mentally, physically, spiritually, and socially—"in wisdom and stature, and in favour with God and man" (Luke 2:52).

Try to see your room as two-year-old Kirk or one-year-old Sue or three-year-old Tim sees it. Does it say "Come in, explore, and have a happy time?" Is it attractive? Is there plenty of space in which Tim or Sue or Kirk may move about? Is it homelike? Is the equipment scaled to the small stature of Tim, Sue, or Kirk? Is your space conveniently located so the child does not have to walk up and down steps or down long halls to "my room"?

The type and amount of equipment, the number of children in the room, the amount of space for each child, the drabness or attractiveness of the room, all contribute to experiences from which the child develops his basic concept of the church. A child learns through association. Therefore, the experiences which he has at church—the pleasure or discomfort he feels in connection with those experiences—will determine the way he feels about the church and will be associated with his learnings about Jesus, God, the Bible, others, and himself.

I. PROVIDING DESIRABLE ROOMS

An attractive room with suitable equipment of the right height and size creates an atmosphere which helps a child to think of the church as a pleasant place.

Small children are active and must move about. This is

41

the way God made them. Small rooms and too many children may cause overstimulation and hostile feelings. These in turn cause behavior problems, such as hitting, biting, pushing, or snatching. Unpleasant experiences are associated with the church. The child may develop the feeling that church is an unpleasant place and resist church attendance. Guiding children in Christian living is best done in rooms planned for the child.

1. Space

Every effort should be made to provide adequate space for children. Better provisions can often be made through rearrangements and remodeling. In some situations the only answer is to erect new buildings.

Every church should plan to minister to babies, toddlers, two-year-olds, and three-year-olds. Wherever possible, a church should provide separate rooms. Large churches will need multiple departments; smaller churches may have only two Nursery rooms; others may not be able to provide more that one room. In such cases dividers are necessary. In planning the space, allow for an increase in enrolment during the year for all Nursery departments.

Babies need space. When a baby can creep about freely on his hands and knees, he does not want to be confined to a bed or playpen all the time. He enjoys the freedom of being on the floor and able to move about.

In many situations when the babies become creepers, they need a room of their own, with workers who understand them and who help them to have experiences on their own level. If left in the room with the babies, the creeper may pull up to the bed, push objects through the rails to the baby, poke and push the baby, and explore the diaper bag hanging nearby. Creepers also make it difficult for workers to move about the room ministering to the babies.

If put in the room with toddlers, a creeper is likely to be

pushed, hit, slapped, or loved too hard. He cannot defend himself. He may even interfere with the movements of the toddlers who are just beginning to be sure of themselves on their feet.

In every Nursery department, room is essential to the child's balanced development. The young child needs space. Actually, the smaller the child moving about the room, the more space he needs. Children need to move. Every muscle calls out for action. Watch a toddler as he goes continually from one place to another in the room. Observe a three-year-old as he works in the home-living area, moves on to look at books, and then on to painting. Sixteen to twenty-five square feet for each person is recommended (preferably twenty-five). More space is desirable.

The diagrams on the next page show why children need space.

2. *Location*

Nursery rooms should be located on the first floor of the building. The rooms, especially those for two- and three-year-olds, should be near bathrooms if toilet facilities are not adjoining them.

The rooms should have clear glass windows about 24 inches from the floor so the children can look out. Window screens should be securely fastened on the outside.

There should be safe exits from all the rooms. Consult your fire department for fire regulations.

If there is plenty of outdoor space and the rooms for the Nursery children are small, the sessions may be held outside when the weather permits. Fence in the needed area. Move basic equipment and materials from the rooms to the fenced-in area. Follow the regular procedure. What better way could a child learn about God than through the things which he sees, feels, tastes, and hears while he is outdoors in God's world.

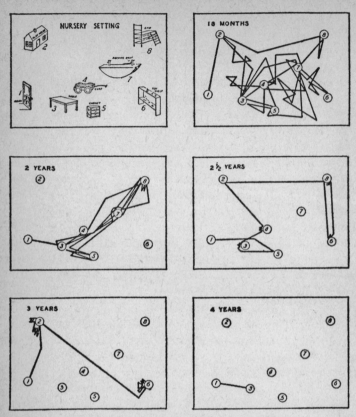

Each diagram represents seven minutes of play.[1]

The equipment shown in the first diagram includes some items which would not be used in a church Nursery department, although they might be found in a secular nursery school. The drawings are included here to show the movements of a typical child at each age in the church Nursery department or elsewhere.

3. *Floor Coverings*

Floors should be covered with material that is easily kept clean, durable, and noise resistant. Such coverings are linoleum, rubber or vinyl tile. Choose a plain or subdued pattern; avoid nursery rhymes and dark colors. Do not use wall-to-wall carpet. Children spend much time working and playing on the floor. Accidents happen, paint is dripped, or water is spilled and must be wiped up. Floors should be cleaned thoroughly each time the room is used.

4. *Lighting*

If the Nursery rooms are located on a southern or eastern exposure and have plenty of windows they will probably have enough natural light during daytime sessions. Be sure there is sufficient artificial light for night sessions. Ask your local light company to check the lighting in each of the rooms.

5. *Heating*

Heating should be so arranged that floors are kept warm and free of drafts. A thermometer in the room near the floor will indicate whether or not the temperature is being maintained at about 68 to 70 degrees. When heaters or radiators must be used, surround them by a low fence or shields to protect the children from burns. There should be good ventilation at all times.

6. *Walls*

Children are influenced by colors, often unconsciously. Drab colors are depressing; harsh, bright colors are agitating; soft, cool colors are soothing and pleasing.

The size, location, and lighting of the room should determine the colors used. Soft shades are best for Nursery rooms. A room with little natural light needs a light color, such as yellow. A cool room, perhaps with a northern exposure, needs a warm color such as a soft peach; a warm room with a southern or western exposure needs a soft, cool blue, or a soft, restful green. Pastel colors make a room appear larger than it is. They have the effect of making the walls stretch out in the distance. Painting one wall a shade deeper than the other three walls also makes the room appear larger, as will painting the woodwork the same color as the walls. Walls should be washable. The colors in walls and floor covering should blend.

7. Supply Cabinets

Supply cabinets on the walls, about fifty inches from the floor and extending to the ceiling, provide storage space. Wall cabinets do not take up the floor space needed for the children.

8. Toilet Facilities

It is desirable to have toilet facilities adjoining the Nursery rooms, especially the rooms for toddlers, two's and three's. All fixtures should be child size. Place the basin approximately 25 inches from the floor. If the bathroom for adults must be used, place a sturdy box or platform under the basin for the child to stand on when washing his hands. A child's toilet seat placed on the commode will keep the child from being afraid of falling into the commode.

9. Reception Areas

Reception areas are not essential; it may be better to put the space into Nursery rooms. The reception area may become a handicap. The doors of the Nursery rooms opening into the area can cause a bottleneck for the parents coming for their children. If parents stop to "socialize" the congestion upsets the children, since they must come out into the group of people. Mothers who are reluctant to leave their children often remain in the reception area rather than going to the departments and classes or unions where they belong.

If there is a reception area, use simple, plain, washable furniture (desk, lamp, and chair). A bulletin board may be used for the display of helpful leaflets, notices to parents, and other information. The fever thermometer and first-aid kit may be in this area.

10. *Kitchenette*

A kitchenette is not necessary. If there is adequate space, a small service area may open off the reception room. It may be equipped with a stove-sink-refrigerator unit. The refrigerator is the most important, since it is needed for the storage of fruit juice or milk for the extended session.

11. *Provision for Wraps*

A movable rack for wraps may be used. The rack may be moved just outside the door if there is space, thus eliminating a lot of confusion when a parent comes for a child between sessions. A worker quietly takes the child to the door, and here the child's wraps are put on after he has left the room. This procedure avoids upsetting the other children, for they do not see the child put on his wraps. The movable rack may be stored during the summer.

For toddlers the rack should be adult height, since these children are unable to hang their own wraps. For two's and three's the rod should be placed low enough to enable the children to hang up their own wraps. Child-size hangers should be used. Hanging up his own coat encourages a child to be independent. If desired, provision may be made in the reception area for adult wraps.

12. *Some Don't's in Planning for Nursery Children*

Don't install loud speakers in any of the Nursery rooms. Workers do not have time to listen to the sermon, for their full attention is given to the learning experiences which the children are having. Parents feel more secure about leaving their children with workers who can give undivided attention to the children.

The loud speaker causes the children to try to talk over the noise and leads to confusion and frustration. The experience may frighten the children, especially the babies and toddlers. The services are beyond the understanding of the children. Further, installing the system is expensive, and the money used for it could be spent more wisely in equipping the rooms for children.

Don't install number or call systems. Very seldom does a worker have to send for a mother. Loving workers know how to help a child to be happy. They are skilled in caring for a child's needs. It is good for a child to have the experience of finding comfort and security through the ministry of the workers, for it helps him to develop a good feeling about "church."

Don't use chalkboards or bulletin boards in any of the Nursery rooms. If desired, a bulletin board may be used in the reception area.

Picture rails are not necessary for Nursery rooms. Pictures may be set on the floor, on a window ledge, or on a piece of equipment easily accessible to the child. A child wants to handle a picture when he looks at it.

In the room for babies, pictures may be placed on the wall by making a loop of masking tape with the sticky side out. This is put on the picture and pushed onto the wall. The picture may be taken down with no damage to the paint.

Don't place pianos in any of the Nursery rooms. They take up valuable space needed for the children. A good record player may be used for listening to music. Workers sing or hum songs to the children. In this way the child hears distinctly the melody and words. Songs are used at any time during the session with an individual child, or with one or

two children. This procedure makes the piano a useless piece
of equipment.

II. PLANNING FOR AGE GROUPING

In many churches the Nursery organizations are deter-
mined by the number of rooms the church assigns them for
use. This may mean merging age groups that would be
better off in separate departments. Consider the diagrams
given in this chapter in determining the best plan for your
Nursery situation.

1. *Four or Five Rooms*

If your church can provide a separate room, or rooms,
for each Nursery department, your space problem is simpli-
fied. Seek to have the needed floor space (preferably 25
square feet per person, if possible). Follow the diagrams
given later in this chapter for a general idea of the arrangement of equipment in each Nursery room. The diagrams also
give some idea of good shape for the various rooms. Avoid
long, narrow rooms. Consider the little child's need for space.
Provide toilet facilities easily accessible to each room.

On the pages which follow, there are diagrams suggesting
possible groupings of departments, room arrangements, and
placement of equipment for churches which cannot provide
a separate room for each Nursery department. Study the
diagrams for suggestions about how to make the most effective use of the space which you can secure for your Nursery work.

In a room for creepers, the equipment will be similar to that
provided for the babies. In addition to beds, there should be
a playpen, a baby jumper, and a Babee-Tenda, if space permits. Diaper bags should be kept out of reach of the creeper.
From time to time *Church Nursery Guide* will offer further
suggestions regarding rooms and equipment for creepers.

2. *Three Rooms*

This sketch shows how to use three rooms for the Nursery group.

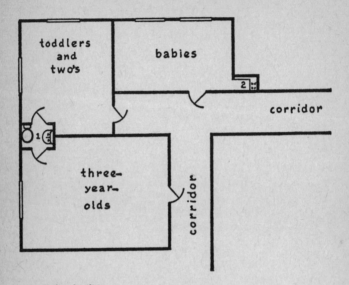

1. Toilet facilities
2. Stove-sink-refrigerator combination

Note the provision for three-year-olds in their own room. Three's can have a brief group time, and can play together much better if there are no younger children in the room.

Babies, too, have individual needs which make it desirable for them to have a room of their own. In the three-room setup, creepers will be placed with babies until they seem mature enough to be classed with toddlers. The number of children in the room for toddlers and two's should be kept below fifteen, if possible. Transfers from room to room may be made as needed during the year.

3. *Two Rooms*

This sketch shows space for Nursery children where only two rooms are available. Note the use of dividers between the space for babies and that for toddlers.

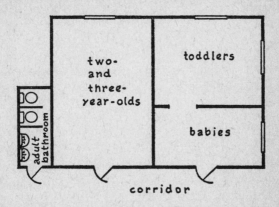

4. *One Room*

There are some churches which can provide only one room for all Nursery children. Where this is true the largest room available should be used.

III. PRINCIPLES OF ROOM ARRANGEMENT

The correct arrangement of equipment and materials will help to create an environment for learning and growing. Consider the following principles:

1. Some materials cause "busy noise" (blocks, home-living). These should not be placed near a quiet activity (books).

2. Materials which require more space (such as blocks) should be placed in a part of the room where the children can spread them out.

3. Materials should not be placed where they interfere with the passing of the children from one activity to another. Do not block passageways. Leave the lanes of traffic free.

4. Place the easel near the bathroom and away from the wall.

5. Arrange equipment so children have enough room to move about it. For example, do not push the stove and cabinet together in the home. Allow room for a child to stand between them.

6. Place the equipment so that it does not jut out into the room and restrict movement. Attention to this point will provide for more room and make it easier for the children to move about.

7. Materials which require good lights, such as books, should be placed in well-lighted areas.

8. Arrange similar materials together (such as all of the home-living materials in one area).

9. Adjust the arrangement to your space. The size of the room will determine what equipment is selected and how it is arranged. Suppose the only room available for three-year-olds is a room 10 by 14 feet. The worker is faced with the problem of providing a good environment for three-year-olds. The amount of equipment must be limited. Choose a doll bed or a rocking chair; stove or table; open shelf for books or blocks or nature materials. The children will sit on the floor, since chairs take up space.

10. Workers should find a good arrangement for their room and leave it. Continual rearrangement of the room upsets the children.

The pages which follow suggest some acceptable room arrangements and equipment appropriate for various Nursery departments. They also show some possible adjustments if ideal space is not available and should offer help which can be adapted by workers in almost any situation.

IV. Suggested Room Arrangements

A ROOM FOR BABIES

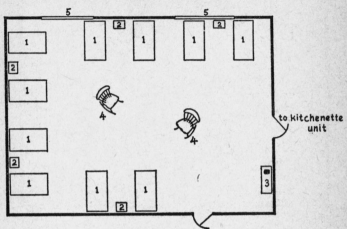

1. Beds
2. Utility tables
3. Table (for Bible and other materials)
4. Rocker
5. Venetian blinds which enable workers to control the light.
6. Many workers prefer a stove-sink-refrigerator combination (not shown) instead of a kitchenette.

Note the easy access to each bed, and the space for a utility table for each two beds. Also note the table for the Bible and other materials, giving prominence and easy access to the Bible for use in the Baby department.

The adult rockers suggest that the babies will have experiences with tender loving care in their church Nursery room. Later concepts of God will be colored by the baby's early feelings of love and security associated with church.

A ROOM FOR TODDLERS

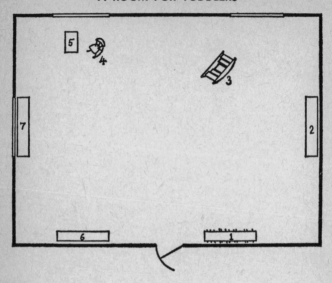

1. Diaper bag shelf and place for wraps
2. Blockbusters
3. Rocking boat and step combination
4. Rocker (child size)
5. Doll bed
6. Bookrack
7. Open shelf for pull toys

The drawing does not show provision for changing diapers. Some workers like to have a table or shelf top for this purpose. Note that the space for diapers is placed out of the toddler's reach. Since he cannot hang up his own wraps, the rack will be of a height for adults to reach.

Note the relative simplicity of equipment. Study the chart and pictures in chapter 2 that show toddler characteristics. How does the equipment suggested in this diagram relate to the needs and abilities of toddlers?

A ROOM FOR TWO-YEAR-OLDS

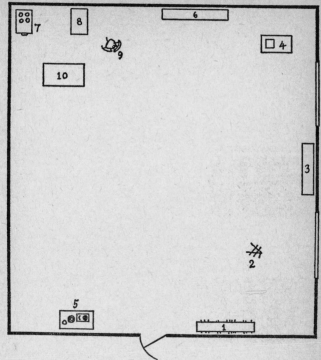

1. Provision for wraps (in reach of child)
2. Easel
3. Bookrack
4. Puzzle table with puzzle
5. Record player
6. Blocks
7. Sink-stove combination (child-size)
8. Doll bed
9. Child's rocker
10. Kitchen table (24″ x 36″ and 20″ high)

A ROOM FOR THREE-YEAR-OLDS

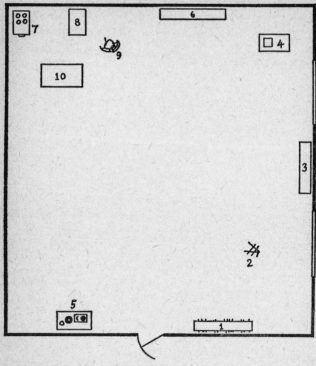

1. Provision for wraps (in reach of child)
2. Easel
3. Bookrack
4. Puzzle table with puzzle
5. Record player
6. Blocks
7. Sink-stove combination (child-size)
8. Doll bed
9. Child's rocker
10. Kitchen table (24" x 36" and 20" high)

IF BABIES, TODDLERS, TWO-, AND
THREE-YEAR-OLDS ARE IN ONE ROOM

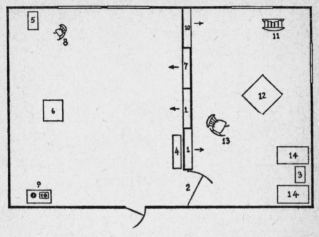

1. Shelves (40 inches high) divide the room. This height prevents children from seeing over the top. The divider is made up of sections of open shelves. Note how the solid backs and open fronts of the shelf sections are alternated.
2. Door same height as shelves (a latch at the top) prevents children's opening the door.

3. Utility table	9. Table with record player
4. Bookrack	10. Open shelf with toys
5. Doll bed	11. Rocking boat
6. Kitchen table	12. Playpen
7. Blocks on open shelf	13. Rocker (adult size)
8. Rocker (child size)	14. Bed for babies

IN THE CORNER OF A ONE-ROOM CHURCH

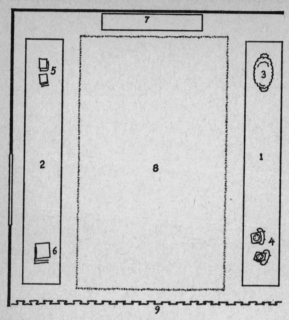

1. and 2. Benches facing each other
3. Bassinet for Baby (if available, a Porta-crib)
4. Two telephones (plastic or wooden)
5. Books
6. Puzzles
7. Small shelf with some toys
8. Washable rug
9. Screen or curtain for divider

Please note that, even in this corner of a one-room church the little child can have many learning experiences. The baby can find love, comfort, and a sense of security in the familiar bassinet each Sunday. The creeper may spend some time on the rug, if the temperature is all right. Older children can have significant experiences as they use the telephones, books, or puzzles. The essential "equipment" is the right Nursery worker, who will help the children to experience desirable learnings, and to associate feelings of love, security, and happiness with everything connected with church.

SUGGESTED ACTIVITIES

For Workers Who Study This Book

1. Make a sketch of your room.
2. Sketch in the present arrangement of the equipment.
3. Study the sketches given in this chapter, then on another sheet of paper, sketch a better arrangement for the equipment in your room.

---

[1] "Reprinted by permission of the Association for Childhood Education International, 1200 Fifteenth Street, N.W., Washington 5, D. C. From *Research Abstracts*, CHILDHOOD EDUCATION, Feb. 1944, Vol. 20, No. 6, page 285—"Locomotor Pathways of Pre-School Children, by Louise Bates Ames, Clinic of Child Development, Yale University."

CHAPTER 4

I. FACTORS TO CONSIDER

    1. Available Space
    2. Durability
    3. Safety
    4. Development of the Child

II. MATERIALS COMMON TO ALL DEPARTMENTS

    1. Bible
    2. Books
    3. Dolls
    4. Pictures
    5. Record Player and Records
    6. Wall Supply Cabinets
    7. Curriculum Materials

III. MATERIALS AND EQUIPMENT FOR BABIES

IV. MATERIALS AND EQUIPMENT FOR CREEPERS AND TODDLERS

V. EQUIPMENT AND MATERIALS FOR TWO- AND
THREE-YEAR-OLDS

4

Selecting Equipment and Materials

NURSERY CHILDREN learn through experiences. The type of experiences they have at church depends upon the environment provided for them. Equipment and materials chosen to meet the needs of the children who are to use them are a part of that environment.

I. FACTORS TO CONSIDER

A number of factors enter into the selection of equipment and materials.

1. *Available Space*

A worker who chooses wisely can still have a good environment for Nursery children even though her space is limited. There are many materials that do not take up much space, but meet the needs of a child, appeal to his interests, and promote growth. One piece of equipment or material may suggest a variety of uses to a child.

2. *Durability*

Any equipment used with Nursery children should be simple, sturdily built, and durable. The natural curiosity of a Nursery child many times leads him to take things apart. There is much handling, tugging, pushing, and pulling of materials by the child.

3. *Safety*

A rigid factor in selecting equipment and materials is safety. Even though a piece of equipment appears to be safe, it can become dangerous if there are knobs and other parts which can be pulled off. Equipment should be without sharp edges or corners, smooth, and free of splinters. Paint used on any materials or equipment should be non-toxic and the kind which does not rub off or crack.

4. *Development of the Child*

Materials should be within the child's realm of experience and level of development. Materials too advanced for a child may discourage his activity and make him discontented. On the other hand, if the material is too simple, the child will not be challenged.

Materials are the tools which a child needs in order to develop. As he uses the materials, situations are created which provide opportunities for him to begin to practice Christian attitudes toward others—sharing, co-operating, considering others, and waiting turns. Such opportunities enable a child to grow toward God, to grow in awareness of himself, and to discover his own world.

The chart included in this chapter lists equipment and materials to meet the needs and interests of each Nursery child. A careful study of the chart should help churches to secure suitable equipment.

II. MATERIALS COMMON TO ALL DEPARTMENTS

Certain basic materials are needed in each department—Baby, Creeper, Toddler, Two-Year, and Three-Year.

1. *Bible*

A Bible 1450BP, available at your Baptist Book Store, has been designed for use with children. A copy should be placed in each Nursery room. The pictures in this Bible were chosen from teaching pictures which have been used with children. The pages of the Bible can be turned by the child. The Bible should not have a thumb index.

2. *Books*

Books for each Nursery age are suggested in the periodicals *Church Nursery Guide* and *Living with Children*. Others are listed in the free booklet "Books for Nursery Children, Parents, and Workers."

3. *Dolls*

Soft, cuddly dolls with painted hair and eyes are best for Nursery children. The doll should be large enough for the child to hold easily in the crook of the arm. It should be made of material which will not be damaged when wiped with a damp cloth. Arms, head, and legs should be securely attached to the body.

4. *Pictures*

The church should provide at least one set of *Church Nursery Pictures* for each room. The set contains twenty pictures chosen especially for the Nursery child. Individual pictures—a few at a time—will be used over and over. The set may be ordered from the Baptist Sunday School Board in the same manner as the lesson periodicals. Pictures cut from magazines and mounted on cardboard may also be used.

Use pictures which a child may touch and hold in his hands, rather than having them attached to the wall. The pictures should be placed on the eye level of the age group with which they are being used—24 to 27 inches from the floor for creepers and toddlers; 27 to 30 inches for two's and three's; and frequently on the bed for the baby.

5. *Record Player and Records*

The record player should have a good tone and play three speeds. See current leaflets and Nursery periodicals for suggested records to be used with each Nursery age group.

6. *Wall Supply Cabinets*

The wall supply cabinets should be placed approximately 50 inches from the floor, to leave the floor for activities.

7. *Curriculum Materials*

Every Nursery worker should have and use the periodical *Church Nursery Guide*. It is designed to guide each worker in becoming a better teacher (1) by helping him in his spiritual growth; (2) by increasing his understanding of Nursery children and abilities in guiding them; (3) by suggesting materials, activities, and experiences to be used with Nursery children to help each one develop a foundation for Christian living; and (4) by helping the worker realize the importance of early religious training for Nursery children.

Church Nursery Guide is used by all Nursery workers in planning for Sunday school and its extended session, Training Union and its extended session, and for weekday activities. Supplementary help, *Daytime and Nighttime*, is provided for those who guide Nursery children during a church study course. Additional units will be offered from time to time.

Even though the periodical *Living with Children* is planned for parents of Nursery children, each worker needs a copy each quarter. Workers need to become acquainted with the contents of the periodical in order to be able to strengthen its use by parents in the home. *Living with Children* is planned to guide parents in becoming better teachers (1) by suggesting ways the home and church can supplement each other in teaching the child; (2) by increasing their understanding of how Nursery children develop religious concepts; (3) by suggesting materials, activities, and experiences to be used in the home (closely related to the suggestions in *Church Nursery Guide*); and (4) by helping parents in their spiritual growth.

Equipment and Materials	BABIES	TODDLERS	TWO'S	THREE'S
Baby's Schedule (card)	x			
Babee-Tenda Safety Chair	x			
Ball (7" or 9" in diameter)	x	x	optional	optional
Beds (hospital cribs, 27" by 42")	x			
Bible (No. 1450BP)	x	x	x	x
Blockbusters (set of 12)		x	x	supplementary
Blocks (set No. 0)			supplementary	x
Blocks (large, wooden, hollow)			optional	optional
Block accessories			x	x
Books (as recommended)	x	x	x	x
Bookrack (28" long and 27" high)		x	x	x
Cabinet on wall for supplies(50" from floor)	x	x	x	x
Chairs (seat 10" from floor)			x	x
Chair (adult rocker, all wood)	x	optional		
Chair (child's, blunt rockers)		optional	x	x
Changing diapers, provision for	(in bed)	x		
Diaper-bag holders (pigeonholes on wall)	x	x		
Dishes (soft plastic)		optional	x	x
Doll (rubber, molded head)	x	x	x	x
Doll bed (16" by 26", and 10" high)		x	x	x
Easel (for painting)			optional	x
Finger paints				x

Equipment and Materials	BABIES	TODDLERS	TWO'S	THREE'S
Modeling dough (Fundo, water clay, or homemade dough)			x	x
Nature materials	x	x	x	x
Newsprint paper			optional	x
Open shelves (two sets, 10" deep, 30" long, and 27" high; movable; closed back)		x	x	x
Paints and brushes			optional	x
Pictures (selected and mounted)	x	x	x	x
Playpen	x	x		
Pull toys		x	x	
Puzzle rack			x	x
Puzzles (wooden)			x	x
Record albums (Broadman)	x	x	x	x
Record player (Voice of Music)	x	x	x	x
Resting cots or mats (for extended session)		x	x	x
Rocking boat and steps combination		x	optional	
Shoofly	optional	x		
Smocks or uniforms for workers (pastel)	x	optional		
Sterilizing solution (Zephiran chloride concentrate, or others)	x	x	x	x
Stove or stove and sink combination (24" high)			x	x
Stove, sink, and refrigerator combination (adult size, 28" by 30" and 40" high)	x			
Swing (Cosco)	x			

Equipment and Materials	BABIES	TODDLERS	TWO'S	THREE'S
Table (24" by 36", and 20" high; usually two)			x	x
Table (utility, Cosco)	x			
Thermometer (room)	x	x	x	x
Toilet (flush bowl, Sani-set, or others)	x			
Toilet (juvenile fixtures)		x	x	x
Transportation toys (interlocking trains, boats, cars, trucks)		x	x	x
Wastepaper basket (plastic)	x	x	x	x

III. MATERIALS AND EQUIPMENT FOR BABIES

Just as older Nursery children respond to an environment, so do babies. The baby is not able to tell a worker in words that the bed is too small or uncomfortable. Nor is he able to say, "I like a clean, attractive room when I come to church." A baby does let a worker know through his behavior, however, how he feels about his room at church. Although Maryann was a six-month-old baby, she was so small and doll-like that the worker decided to put her in a smaller bed and save the larger bed for other babies. Maryann began to cry when the worker put her in the bed. This response was most unusual. The worker could not determine what was wrong. She decided to try an experiment. Maryann was put in a larger bed. Immediately she stopped crying and looked up smiling. She needed room and her cry was her only means of telling her need.

Beds should be safe, sanitary, and attractive for the baby. They should be of good construction, convenient height, easy to adjust, and clean. The best beds are hospital cribs, 27 inches by 42 inches, which can be bought from surgical supply houses. If hospital cribs cannot be secured, a similar type of bed should be used. A bed the same size as the hospital crib is desirable. Larger beds take up too much space; smaller ones crowd the children.

Avoid using built-in beds. They place the babies too close to each other. As a child begins to pull up, he can reach the baby next to him. Trouble may result. Built-in beds are inconvenient for the adult caring for the baby. If the beds are placed three feet apart, workers have space in which to care for the baby. Each time the beds are used, wash them with soap and water or a sterilizing solution.

Hospital Crib

Bottle warmers may be secured locally. Even though there is a kitchenette close by, some workers prefer to have one or two bottle warmers in the room, since unnecessary leaving of the department is to be discouraged.

Toys (rubber or plastic) should be those that appeal to a baby. Be sure there is no extra button, ribbon, or part which the baby can pull off. The toys should be those which can be sterilized after each use or after they are dropped. Examples of toys that appeal to a baby are a Cradle Gym,

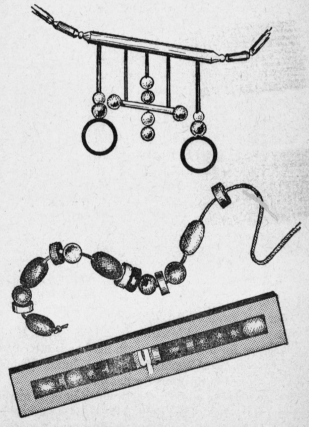

Cradle Gym and Baby Beads (plastic)

baby beads, hand-gripping rattle, beach or rubber balls, and rubber dolls without hair, eyelashes, or movable eyes.

Encourage each mother to bring one of her baby's own toys to church with him. The familiar object helps in giving him a feeling of security.

Diaper bags for babies may be placed in small wire baskets suspended under each bed, or in a diaper tray of light weight wood (made by a local carpenter). If any babies in the room are allowed on the floor, other provisions need to be made for diaper bags.

Shelves (for diaper bags) may be built on the wall in one section of the room. This arrangement is inconvenient, however, for some workers must walk the length of the room each time the baby is diapered.

Be sure each diaper bag and all items in the bag are labeled with the child's name. Encourage parents to do the labeling before bringing the diaper bag. Keep masking or adhesive tape close by to label items in case the parent forgets. A Magic Marker or pen may be used to put the name on the tape.

Rocking chairs of adult size are used by workers. At least one is needed for each Baby department. If space permits, another rocker may be added. Some workers prefer rockers without arms. Use rockers with wooden seats instead of fabric.

A *utility table* (Cosco) may be placed between each two beds for diaper bags and supplies. If there is not adequate space for this arrangement, one table may be moved from place to place and used in caring for all the babies. If there is not a place for a worker to wash her hands after caring for a baby, a basin of Zephiran chloride solution should be placed on a table in the room for this purpose.

Sheets, preferably contour sheets which fit each mattress and so keep the baby from pulling the sheet out, should be supplied. At least two changes of sheets will be needed for each bed. Sheets should be changed each time the bed is used. Sometimes they will need to be changed more than once during a session.

Sterilizing solutions, such as Zephiran chloride concentrate or Roccal Sanitizing Agency, may be used for sterilizing toys, books, and beds. These sterilizers may be purchased at the drugstore. If Zephiran chloride concentrate is used, put two tablespoons of the chemical in one gallon of water. In sterilizing toys, immerse them in the solution. It is not necessary to rinse or dry them. Soap and water may also be used effectively for sterilization.

Uniforms may be wrap-around dresses, smocks, or pinafores. They may be made by the workers or purchased at a department store or your Baptist Book Store. Men who work in the Baby department may wear uniforms similar to those worn by doctors and dentists. Some workers prefer pastel shades because they feel that babies may be afraid of the white uniform, if they associate it with unhappy experiences.

Other materials consist of disposable diapers, towels, washcloths, cotton, cleansing tissues, rectal thermometer for taking temperature, oil, and powder. If there is adequate space, a swing, playpen, or a baby jumper (Cosco Baby Jumper preferred) may be added to the room, for older babies who do not enjoy staying in the bed all of the time.

IV. MATERIALS AND EQUIPMENT FOR CREEPERS AND TODDLERS

When a child begins to move about the room either by crawling, creeping in some way, or beginning to walk, he becomes a creeper. When the child has developed to the point that he is steady on his feet, he is known as a toddler. There is not a set age at which a child becomes a creeper or a toddler; each child reaches that stage of development at his own rate.

It is best for creepers and toddlers to have separate rooms. However, this may be impossible because of lack of space.

The space and number of children in a room will determine whether or not the creeper will remain in the room with babies or be transferred to the room for toddlers.

The creeper and toddler find their world exciting with so many things to explore, to feel, to touch, to taste, to see. Pushing and pulling are newly acquired abilities. The creeper and toddler have to try them out.

Caution needs to be exercised in selecting equipment and materials for these age groups. A creeper or toddler will continue to try to put everything in his mouth to get the taste of it and the feel of it. If anything can be pulled apart, the toddler will pull it apart. Equipment and materials must be durable and safe.

The *safety chair, swing, shoofly,* and *playpen* are for babies approaching the creeping stage, who fret against staying in bed. These babies may be transferred to the room for creepers and put in a playpen or other piece of equipment. If creepers and toddlers are together, such equipment provides a safe place for the child who does not get around easily. From time to time, creepers will enjoy being in the swing or shoofly. Sometimes a toddler will find security in the playpen.

Shoofly

A *bed* is needed in the room for creepers for the child who goes to sleep. However, one is not needed in the room for toddlers. If a toddler goes to sleep, he may be placed in a playpen bed or on a mat or rug on the floor. It is best to keep him in his regular room. Moving a child from one room to another can be upsetting to him.

Blockbusters used by toddlers are sturdy, indoor, hollow blocks made of heavy carton stock. The inside is reinforced with strong material to enable a child to sit on the blocks or walk on them. These can be purchased from your Baptist Book Store.

For diaper bag holders for toddlers, open shelves high on the wall are divided into sections, each of which is marked with a child's name. Allow extra sections for visitors and for children who are brought to church irregularly. Keep tape and pen close at hand so workers can quickly place a child's name on an empty section. Encourage parents to put the child's name on his diaper bag and on all the contents.

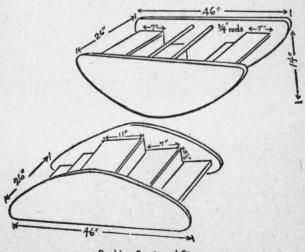

Rocking Boat and Steps

A *combination rocking boat and steps* (if there is floor space) may be used in the room for toddlers. Upright, this piece of equipment is a set of steps to satisfy the child's desire for climbing. When turned over, it becomes a rocking boat large enough for two to four children.

Nature materials, such as bulbs, vines, flowers, turtles, leaves, goldfish, birds, fruits, shells, rocks, and vegetables provide opportunities for tasting, handling, and smelling.

Open shelves (30 inches long, 27 inches high, 10 inches deep) for educational toys in the room for toddlers. Having a place for the materials encourages the child to put away what he uses and gives him a greater feeling of security. Shelves are not needed for Blockbusters, as they may be stacked on the floor.

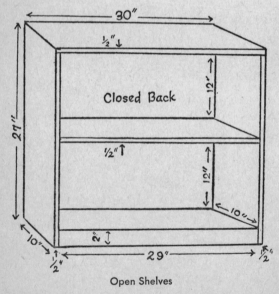

Open Shelves

A *bookrack* with slanting shelves has several advantages. A child can easily see the front of the books when they are placed on the slanting shelves. When books are set up on open shelves, there is a tendency for them to warp; placing them on slanting shelves prevents this. It is easier for the child to put a book back on a slanting shelf than to set it upright on an open shelf. Bookracks may be purchased from the Baptist Book Store or made by a local carpenter.

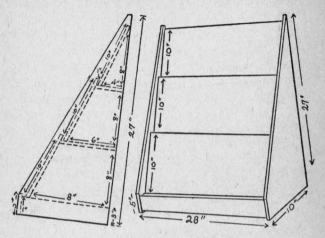

Bookrack—Front and Side View

Resting mats or cots are to be used during the extended session with toddlers. A cot is better for resting than a mat, for the cot encourages the child to relax. It conveys the idea of a bed, which to the child means resting and sleeping. Light aluminum cots, which can be stacked conveniently, may be purchased from educational equipment companies. If cots cannot be secured, large heavy bath towels, bath mats, or small individual rugs are satisfactory.

Telephones should be made of soft plastic and be washable and unbreakable. Having two telephones enables the toddler to talk with a worker or with another child. There should be a doll bed sturdy enough for a child to crawl in and out of, if he wishes. The bed may be made by a local carpenter or purchased through the nearest Baptist Book Store.

Creepers and toddlers need toys which they can push, pull, fill, and dump, such as plastic dishpans, corrugated boxes, or a wooden floor train with interlocking sections. Other toys should be available such as rubber balls (5 inches to 7 inches in diameter—medium size beach balls may be used because of their lightness); at least two washable rubber dolls without hair, eyelashes, or movable eyes. The toddler cannot dress or undress a doll; he will use a blanket in which to wrap the doll. Toys should be well constructed, with parts that do not pull off. Avoid pins and ribbons.

Miscellaneous materials are cleansing tissues, sponges, and a wastepaper basket.

V. EQUIPMENT AND MATERIALS FOR TWO- AND THREE-YEAR-OLDS

Two- and three-year-olds will use some materials and equipment similar to that listed for toddlers, but the usage will show more maturity. Children learn best through experience. Equipment that may be adapted to various uses will suggest many possibilities to the two's and three's and provide valuable experiences for them. Most of the equipment may be purchased through the Baptist Book Store, or manufacturers of children's toys (see chapter 9), or be made by a local carpenter. Study the chart and the pictures in this chapter for suggestions.

A movable open shelf for blocks (10 inches deep, 30 inches long, and 27 inches high, with closed back) encourages the child to get the blocks for himself and to put them back when he has finished. If desired, another shelf unit may be placed in the room for other materials. A good supply of blocks of different shapes and sizes is needed. Educational Blocks, Set No. 0, are recommended. If the blocks are made by a local carpenter, be sure they are sanded until very smooth, and all edges rounded. Blocks may be shellacked if desired. Do not paint them.

Other materials, such as wooden figures (animals, family, helpers), cars, a truck, floor train, may be added to make working with blocks more fascinating.

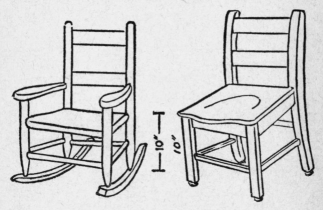

Child's Chair and Rocker

Chairs 10 inches high from the floor are provided for three-year-olds. These should be comfortable and not easily turned over. Provide only enough chairs for the average attendance. Extra chairs take up valuable space.

Since two-year-olds do not have group time, the only chairs needed are in the home-living area and at the table where puzzles and recordings are used. Frequently, a child sits on the floor or stands to work a puzzle. A child-size rocker with blunt rockers should be placed in the home-living area. If there is space, two rockers may be used.

If an adult feels the need for a chair, use one 10 inches high. Avoid the use of adult chairs, since workers tend to become spectators when they are above the child's level.

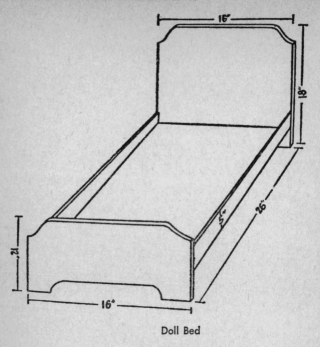

Doll Bed

A *doll bed* sturdy enough for a child to sit on or lie down in can be used, even when space is limited.

A *double easel* (36 inches high for two-year-olds and 40 inches high for three-year-olds) provides a painting area. Newsprint (18 inches by 24 inches) clipped to the painting surface of the easel enables the child to make big movements. Newsprint may be bought at a local office supply store. Many times the local newspaper plant will give away or sell for a small amount of money the newsprint left after each printing of the paper.

Brushes with long handles and one-inch-wide bristles, powder tempera paint, and paint containers (glasses, jars, milk cartons, or plastic glasses) complete the materials for painting.

Double Easel

Tables (not more than two, 24 by 36 inches, 20 inches high) are needed. Use one in the home-living area. Tables should have washable tops (Formica or plastic).

A *stove* (child size) may be used with both two's and three's. It may be made by a local carpenter or bought.

A *cabinet-sink* combination may be used in both the Two- and Three-Year departments. This provides a place for dishes and cooking utensils in the home-living area. A rod may be attached to the side for dish cloths, towels, and aprons.

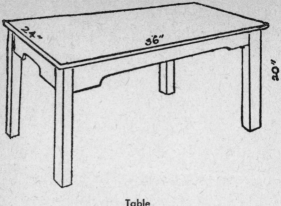

Table

A *puzzle rack* provides a place for the puzzles which all children enjoy. Its use will prevent the scratching of the puzzles and losing of pieces.

Since two-year-olds lack the co-ordination necessary for putting the puzzles in and taking them out of the rack, it is wise to put those the children are to use on a table. Workers will be responsible for putting the puzzles away in the puzzle rack.

The wall supply cabinet (p. 82) should be fastened to the wall near the door. The bottom of cabinet should be about 4 feet 2 inches from the floor. The top of the cabinet may extend to the ceiling. Adjustable shelves within the cabinet are desirable, since they can be spaced to accommodate materials of various sizes.

The rack for children's wraps (p. 82) should be movable. It may be placed under the supply cabinet. If space permits, the rack may be used in the hall near the door. The shelf is of wood. The hollow pipes used in making the rack are durable and economical. The plates and pipes are threaded and can be adjusted in height, or for leveling.

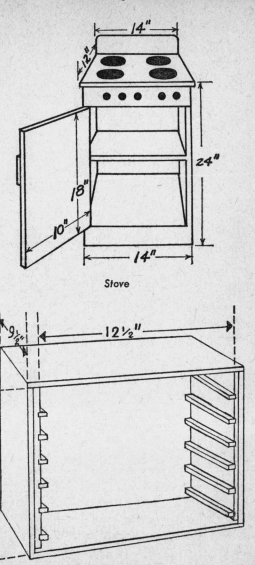

Stove

Puzzle Rack

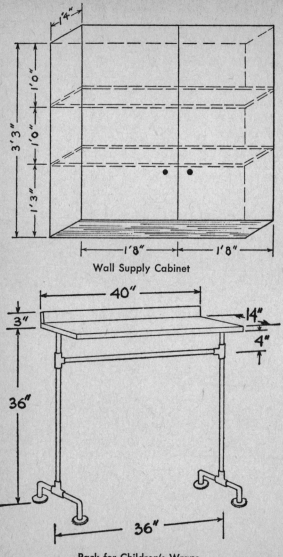

Wall Supply Cabinet

Rack for Children's Wraps

Nature materials, such as plants, animals, minerals, seasonal objects, goldfish, or a dish garden, may be placed on an open shelf or in low windows, where they can be examined and handled by the children.

Miscellaneous materials consist of dishes (soft plastic), cooking utensils (child size), rolling pins, dolls without hair and movable eyes, doll clothes, doll blankets and sheets, child-size suitcase for doll blankets and clothes, "dress-up" clothes, carton of plastic or wooden milk bottles, first-aid kit, waste basket, cleansing tissue, and sponges.

SUGGESTED ACTIVITIES

For Workers Who Study This Book

1. List the materials and equipment in your department.
2. List in a parallel column the additional materials and equipment you would like to have.
3. Think about your available space and the number of children enrolled in your department. Ask this question about each piece of material and equipment which you have listed in the two columns: "Can this piece of material (equipment) be used in the space we now have without crowding the children?"
4. List the material and equipment to which you can say "yes" to the question above. This is the needed equipment for your department now. What needs to be discarded?

CHAPTER 5

Materials for Learning Experiences

FOUNDATIONS FOR Christian personality begin in early childhood. Even for the baby, present experiences are shaping his feeling about God, Jesus, the Bible, church, others, self.

I. NURSERY TEACHING OBJECTIVES

Nursery workers seek to help each child have experiences that will aid in his growth toward a mature Christian personality. The over-all purpose is to meet his needs, especially his spiritual needs, through making him feel comfortable and happy, loved and wanted, secure and unhurried. These feelings furnish a positive basis for the development of right attitudes.

1. *General Statement*

Nursery workers are achieving this over-all purpose when they guide each child in experiences that will help him to—

GROW in his *independence* in meeting and solving his own problems; make progress in sharing and taking turns;

FEEL more *secure* with adults, with other children, and in a variety of situations;

BEGIN to associate *God* with feelings of wonder, love, and happiness, and with the many happy experiences; want to talk to God in his own way;

FEEL that *Jesus* loves him; feel that Jesus loves others;

THINK of the *Bible* as a special book; to become familiar with and enjoy Bible stories that are meaningful to him (related to his own experiences);

THINK of his *church* as a special place where the family may go to learn more about God and Jesus; to have happy experiences with friendly people at "my church";

THINK of his *home* as a place where he is loved and wanted; have happy experiences at home where he can work and play with others.

2. Objectives in Various Areas of Learning

Nursery objectives may be stated in terms of the areas of learning involved.

(1) *About God.*—A child soon begins to have thoughts and feelings about God when he senses that God is real and important to those who work with him. Their expressions of love, thoughtfulness, and forgiveness become a part of the child. His interest in nature and his feeling of wonder about it make possible his association of God with the world of nature. Hearing and seeing workers talk to God, even though the child does not understand the words, arouses feelings about prayer, and as a result, the child's desire to talk to God will grow.

(2) *About Jesus.*—Listening to stories about Jesus, talking and singing about him, and associating with Christian workers are experiences which help a child to grow in his knowledge and appreciation of Jesus. Through hearing references to the love and helpfulness of Jesus and seeing in workers Christlike personalities, a child gradually comes to think of Jesus as one who is a friend, who loves children, and whom children love. Thus the child begins to lay the foundation for the time when he comes to know Jesus as his personal Saviour.

(3) *About the Bible.*—When workers handle the Bible carefully and say by gesture and by tone of voice that this Book means something special to them, a child begins to think of the Bible as a special book.

(4) *About church.*—Through satisfying experiences at church, a child comes to think of the church as a pleasant place where he learns about God and Jesus.

(5) *About others.*—Each child's world centers about himself. But into that world come people whom he must consider and to whom he must adjust. Workers can help him gradually to become aware of the needs and rights of others by showing this concern themselves and by providing experiences which help the child learn to play happily alone and with others, to use materials constructively, to be successful in his undertakings, to be willing to share, and to be kind to people and animals.

(6) *About self.*—As the little child gradually develops self-awareness, he needs to feel a sense of acceptance.

Such experiences as these—of being loved and respected, of building a sense of adequacy, of feeling worth-while and acceptable to the people with whom you live—have been a part of every child who is outgoing, friendly, eager for new experiences, willing to try the untried, able to approach strange adults and other children with confidence. This is the beginning of a child's trust in other people, thus opening one of the channels by which he comes to God.[1]

II. MATERIALS FOR LEARNING EXPERIENCES

If children are to change in what they think, the way they act, and what they feel, they must be involved personally in experiences which bring about the changes.

A child is not born with the ability to think or reason already developed. God has planned that there be a gradual development of this ability. Such development is based on experiences with materials. As the child faces a problem and works through it to a satisfying conclusion, he is setting up guideposts which will influence his approach to solving problems. As his handling of materials leads him to think of God as the one who makes beautiful things, the child can be led to become personally involved in an experience of worship. What materials will provide these and other learning experiences?

1. *Using the Bible*

Each Nursery department should have its own Bible, since the Bible is used with the baby as well as with the oldest Nursery child.

There is no set place for the Bible in a room. Sometimes it is on the table in the home-living area; at other times it may be near the blocks or with books, or on the shelf with the push-and-pull toys. The worker places the Bible where it can be seen and handled easily and where it will catch and stimulate the interest of a child. She follows this interest by singing, talking about the picture, using story conversation or a story, or talking to God about the Bible. There will be times when a worker does not put the Bible in a particular place, but places it in her lap and opens it to a picture.

Children need help in handling the Bible. Study *Church Nursery Guide* for positive suggestions to use, for example: "Hold the Bible this way." "Turn the pages carefully." "Show me where to put the Bible." All Nursery workers should agree on the same instructions to be used in guiding the children.

As a worker with three-year-olds uses a Bible verse or tells a story, she often says, "It is right here in the Bible," or "The Bible tells us about Jesus." Many times the child wants to "see where it is."

Sometimes a worker plays the game, "I can open the Bible and read," with a child. She opens the Bible and says, "I open the Bible (open to a picture). What do you see?" The child tells in his own words what he sees in the picture.

In conversation workers refer to the Bible. Mrs. Christian brought flowers for some of the three-year-olds to arrange. "Smell the flowers. The Bible says that God made the flowers. It says 'God . . . made every thing' " (Eccl. 3:10-11).

A worker always opens the Bible to the correct reference as she tells a Bible story. One Sunday morning during group time in a Three-Year department, Mrs. Sims opened the Bible to Genesis 1 and said, "In the Bible there is a story about the daytime and the nighttime." Then she told the story.

The following Sunday she opened the Bible to an entirely different place. "Right here," she said, "is a story about daytime and nighttime."

"That isn't where you had it last Sunday," piped a small voice.

At times workers may use their own Bibles and so help the children to see that Bibles do vary in size, color, and use of pictures.

USING THE BIBLE

What do the pictures on this and the following page tell you about the experiences which children of various ages may have as the Bible is used?

As you study each picture, note the role of the worker in helping the child have a meaningful experience.

Note the position of the book in relation to the child's eyes and hands.

Consider the evidences of a child's development in ability to handle the Bible for himself as he progresses from the baby to the three-year stage.

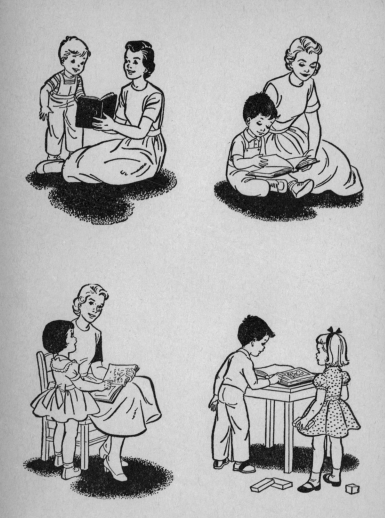

2. *Using Pictures*

Each Nursery department should have its own set of *Church Nursery Pictures*. Other pictures may be found in magazines, catalogs, advertising booklets, and on calendars. Select these pictures carefully. Be sure they have little or no background interest, contain familiar objects within the child's realm of experience (daddy, mother, baby, foods, playthings, houses, clothing, pets, boy, girl, children playing with each other or helping, helpers children know), and have good color. The pictures should be cut out carefully and pasted on cardboard, 8½ by 12 inches. Use strong, transparent paste that is quick to dry and has good sticking quality. File the mounted pictures with the set of *Church Nursery Pictures*.

On the back of each picture in the upper left-hand corner put the number of the classification under which the picture is filed. The classifications of pictures may be similar to this:

1. Jesus	5. Helpers
2. Bible Friends	6. Playing
3. Bible	7. Nature
4. Church	8. Home

File the pictures lengthwise to prevent wrinkling. Write or type a list of the picture classifications and numbers and paste it on the lid of the box. Use the numbers on the dividers in the box.

Suppose Mrs. Jones needs a picture about going to church. She looks on the written or typed sheet on the lid of her picture file and sees that No. 4 has pictures about church. She goes immediately to the section marked No. 4 and finds the picture. After the session, she looks on the back of the picture for the classification number and drops the picture back into section No. 4.

When children say, "Let me see," they mean "Let me take it in my hands and feel it." Because of this, pictures need to be durable, easy to keep clean, and easy for the child to handle. Spray each picture with plastic spray, or use clear shellac or varnish to prevent them from getting dirty. Pictures which have been sprayed may be wiped off with a damp cloth. Pictures may also be preserved by the use of plastic transparent protectors, which may be bought at a book store or variety store.

Pictures speak a language which a child understands. They tell the story on his level. No words have to be used, for pictures tell their own story. As the child looks at the picture, he identifies himself with the action he sees taking place. From a picture he may learn ideas, attitudes, and actions. Pictures clarify words for the child and enlarge his world.

Workers use pictures with babies as well as with the oldest Nursery child. For each session a few pictures may be placed on the floor, in a chair, on a window ledge, on a table, or in the bookrack. A child wants to pick up a picture as he looks at it.

For example, the baby is shown a picture of a glass or bottle of milk. The baby pats and holds the picture. The worker says, "Milk, um-m-m. Good milk. Thank you, God, for milk." If the baby does not show any interest, the worker does not press him. She talks about the pictures in which he shows interest. (She watches for the child's readiness for such activities.)

As a worker shows the baby a picture in the Bible, in a book, from a magazine, or from the *Church Nursery Pictures*, she may sing a song, use story conversation, or talk about the picture.

When a toddler shows an interest in a picture, the worker may talk about the picture (being careful to use few words, and then only those familiar to the child), use story conversation, sing a song, or use a Bible verse. There will be times when the worker will let the child look at the picture independently and make no comments.

Pictures for two- and three-year-olds offer many teaching opportunities. A picture may remind both child and worker of a song or a Bible verse or a Bible story. Sometimes a game is played with a picture. "I see a picture of a boy putting on his shoes all by himself. Do you see a picture of a boy putting on his shoes all by himself? Do you put your shoes on all by yourself like the boy does?" Pictures placed near an activity may suggest ideas for using the materials. The picture, *Dusting with Mother* (No. 4, *Church Nursery Pictures*), placed in the home-living area may suggest dusting the furniture there.

3. Using Books

Experiences with books should be a part of the child's life at church. The books should be of such size that they can be handled easily by the children (8 inches by 8 inches), durable, and with pictures that are clear, have little or no background, and include objects or activities familiar to the child. For babies and toddlers choose durable, washable books made of plastic, linen, cloth, or heavy cardboard. The pictures should consist of only one object each, clear and large enough for the children to enjoy.

The worker may hold the book where the baby can see it, or when he is ready she may put him on his stomach and place the book in front of him, resting it against the head of the bed. She may say, if she has turned to a picture of a dog, "God made the dog."

With a toddler, the worker may carry on a story conversation about the pictures in a book, helping the toddler to identify himself with them. "Kitty. Kitty says 'Meo-ow-ow.' Steve has a kitty. Steve's kitty says, 'Meo-ow-ow.'"

The two-year-old is interested in himself more than anyone else. It is only natural that his favorite book character is someone about his age, who does what he does. He likes stories which revolve around the simple incidents of taking a bath, crawling into bed, drinking a glass of milk, or putting on his shoes. To the two-year-old, putting words to objects is an exciting game.

As a child turns the pages of a book, a worker may use story conversation or play "I See" games. Looking at some books may lead naturally to the telling of a Bible story. At other times looking at a book may lead the worker to sing a song.

Too often workers do all the talking. They should give the child an opportunity to tell what he sees in the pictures of the book first, and, if clarification is needed, then add their brief comment.

The attention span of a two-year-old is short. The worker will be familiar enough with a book and its pictures to either "read" the picture or tell an on-the-spot picture story. Usually when a two-year-old says, "Wead," he is interested in turning the pages and looking at the pictures.

Children enjoy "reading" books to themselves. Or they may simply enjoy looking at the pictures. Workers need to be aware of times when children want to look at books

independently. When a three-year-old child brings a book to the worker saying, "Read this to me," it is an invitation to the worker to share the book with the child.

Hearing a book read may suggest to the child playing the experience. He will do this very simply.

As children look at books, there may be an opportunity to use a Bible verse or song or lead the child in a moment of worship.

Sometimes a book may be read in group time to the three-year-olds. If this is done, the worker should know the book so well that she can "read" it to the children while she turns pages with the book turned toward the children for them to see.

See *Church Nursery Guide* and the leaflet "Books for Nursery Children, Parents, and Workers" for a list of books which may be used with Nursery children, and for suggestions about how to use them.

4. *Using Music*

Children respond to music. It is something in which each child can be an active participant. As the ear becomes keenly attuned to the music, the sounds are transferred to the child's muscle and nerve fibers, and a deep emotional experience results. The child feels happy or sad, pleased or displeased, quiet or active.

Sometimes a child responds to the experience by active physical expression, such as the baby's kicking and smiling and the three-year-old's running. Sometimes the responses are both vocal and active physical expression. Music cannot be separated from activities. It is interwoven in a child's experiences. A child may have a musical experience anywhere, any time while he is at church. He hears a worker singing softly about Jesus and feelings are aroused. The word Jesus is associated with these feelings. Thus the child begins to form concepts of Jesus as someone special, who loves children and whom children love. This developing concept becomes a part of the child's growth toward Jesus.

"Pretty" music is played on the record player. Happy, pleasant feelings are created within the child. Church is associated with happy, pleasant feelings.

(1) *Listening to music.*—A good record player and a few good recordings are a must for each Nursery department. Beautiful music, such as "Cradle Song" by Brahms, helps to quiet the crying baby, soothe the tired one, and give a feeling of contentment and happiness to others. Choose recordings of good classical music with the rich, deep tones of the organ, or the lilting tones of a violin, or the blended tones of an orchestra.

Some recordings which may be used are "Pastoral Symphony," from *The Messiah,* Handel; "Air for G String," Bach; *Nutcracker Suite,* Tschaikovsky; selections from Beethoven's and Brahms' symphonies. These recordings may be used with all Nursery children. The Broadman albums, *Songs for Tiny Tots* and *Songs for Our Littlest Ones* should be used by parents and workers with toddlers, two's, and three's. These albums may be purchased from the Baptist Book Store. Other records which may be used are "Barcarolle" by Offenbach, for rest time, and Pram records for toddlers (5A—"Clap Hands" and "Up, Up, Up"; 1A—"By-Bye" and "Nice"; 2A—"Where Are Your Eyes?" and "Big and Little").

The record player and records may be placed on a low table (approximately 20 inches high) where the children can use them. They may be put on the floor, if a table is not available. Be sure to place the record player where children can listen undisturbed by others.

Children need guidance in using the record player, although many three-year-olds have learned to operate record players of their own.

"Hold the record this way" (between the two index fingers).

"Put the record here" (on turntable).

"Now you are ready to turn it on. Right here." (Indicate knob for turning on the player.)

"Put your finger on this knob and push it this way."

"See, the record goes round and round."

"You can take the record off and turn it over. Then put it back on and we'll listen to the music on the other side."

"Hear the pretty music."

In the same way help a child to know how to take the needle off, place it on the resting place, turn the player off, and take off the record.

A child will need to be reminded at times how to use the player. To avoid the misuse of records, say, "Leave the records here until you are ready to play them."

Two-year-old Dale and a worker sat on the floor by the record player. "What does this say?" asked Dale, holding up a record taken from the album *Songs for Tiny Tots*. The worker told him. Dale carefully put the record on the turntable and turned on the player. The worker put the needle on the record. This went on, with Dale asking each time, "What does this say?" until the entire album had been played. Sometimes Dale just listened to the record. At other times he joined in with the singer. His interest and attention were maintained over an unusually long period for a two-year-old.

(2) *Using songs.*—Music belongs with activity. Children engaging in satisfying activities sing as they work. Children can hear more clearly the tones of the adult voice (which communicates to the child a worker's feelings) if it is not teamed with the piano.

Songs for a Nursery child should be simple, short, and within the understanding of the child. Melodies should be simple, moving in scalewise tones (consecutive). There should be much repetition.

Study this song, which is used with toddlers as they walk up and down the steps:

Up, Up, Up the Steps

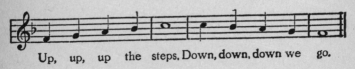

Up, up, up the steps. Down, down, down we go.

Six words are used in the song: up, the, steps, down, we, go. Two words, up and down, are repeated three times each, as the child walks up one side and down the other. Notice the five-note interval—*f* to *c*.

Songs may be made longer by adding another name, food, or animal, and thus making an additional stanza. Notice the song illustrated on the next page.

What are other ways in which a child may help? He can help to plant the seeds, to dry the dishes, to set the table, or to water the flowers. Add these to the song. Not all the stanzas would be sung to the child at one time—only those that fit naturally into the activity.

Workers need to learn many songs. They need to know a song for every occasion and every situation. Often a worker will make up a song or encourage a child to make up a song about a meaningful experience.

I Can Help

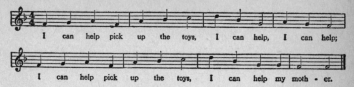

I can help pick up the toys, I can help, I can help;

I can help pick up the toys, I can help my moth - er.

Workers choose songs which contain ideas and experiences familiar to the child (picking up toys, going to church, feeding pets, talking to God, singing about Jesus).

They are careful not to select songs in which words familiar to the child are used as symbols to convey another idea or meaning. For example, the word "light" in "This Little Light of Mine" means to the adult living a Christlike life in a world of sin. The word "light" to the child may suggest the electric light found in his home. Children are literal minded. Suitable songs are found in *Church Nursery Guide*. (Songs in this chapter have been taken from this periodical.)

SUGGESTED ACTIVITIES

For Workers Who Study This Book

1. What are the teaching objectives for the Nursery child in relation to himself, others, and the church?
2. List all the ways of which you can think to help a child learn about God, Jesus, the Bible, the church, others, and self. Draw a line through any way you have listed which does not pass the following tests:
   Within the child's understanding
   Suitable for age group
3. From the discussion of the use of music in this chapter, what reasons can you find why a piano is not recommended?

[1] Phoebe Anderson, *Religious Living with Nursery Children* (Boston: The Pilgrim Press, 1956), p. 25. Used by permission.

CHAPTER 6

6

Materials for Learning Experiences

(Continued)

THE ATTENTION span of a Nursery child is very short. He likes to do many things during the time he is at church. It is necessary to work with each individual or with small groups.

Each child is free when he enters the room to choose the materials he will use. These are the physical tools which he needs to help him grow toward God, to grow as a person, and to become a part of his world. As a child builds with the blocks, he learns that there are other people in the Nursery room. They are people just his size. They, too, want to use the blocks. This experience is the beginning of sharing and developing a sense of property rights. As a child moves from one activity to another, he learns he must adjust to others. He must wait his turn for the book or the paints or the puzzle that someone else is using.

Looking at a book, listening to a worker sing or tell a story, or talking about a nature object can cause a child to feel God's nearness and create a desire to talk to him. These moments of worship, though fleeting, help a child to feel God's love and care.

I. USING STORIES

The gap between a child and his surroundings can be bridged by stories. The three-year-old hearing a story becomes the "story child." The two-year-old finds in stories

101

"new things" for his growing store of knowledge about his world.

The baby or the toddler listening to story conversation is storing up feelings and reactions which color his day-to-day experiences.

The worker is an important factor in storytelling. Feelings about God, Jesus, the church, other people, the world, and the children are reflected by the storyteller and caught by the child.

1. Characteristics of Stories for Nursery Children

Listen to the two's and three's make up stories about themselves. What characteristics do their stories lead you to look for in selecting your stories?

(1) Familiar experiences
(2) Repetition
(3) Words within the child's understanding
(4) Within the child's attention span

The world of the Nursery child revolves about himself. What Bill or May or John does, sees, feels, or wants are the experiences which each one knows. Through these experiences the child deepens his relationship to those in his family, those outside of his family, and those within and outside his church. The Nursery child's stories center around his familiar everyday experiences. The stories are repeated over and over.

2. Using a Story with an Individual Child

A story may be used with one child at a time, when a worker feels that a story fits the situation. Watching the snowflakes float lazily down to the ground or listening to the rain on the windowpane with a child may create an opportunity for a story. Often, the worker will need to make up an on-the-spot story to fit the situation.

3. Using a Story at Group Time

Some three-year-olds can have a short group time. When they do, the worker may or may not use a story. If she does, she observes these simple rules:

1. Sit on the level with the children—have "eye to eye" contact.
2. Tell the story so that each child feels it.
3. Adapt the story to the vocabulary and understanding of the child. Keep the Bible open to the correct reference, if a Bible story is told.
4. Use words with which the children are familiar.
5. Know the story—make it a part of you.

II. Using Paints

A young child learns very little from words alone. He must have firsthand experience for learning. He must have a chance to relive this experience, to play with it, and to express it in various ways. This is not a haphazard way of learning. It is not an optional procedure which a worker may follow or reject. It is the God-planned way for the child to learn.

A child has a deep desire to express himself. Because of his limited vocabulary, most of his thoughts and his feelings cannot be put into words. Many times feelings come out in motor activity, such as biting, hitting, or pushing. A child needs an acceptable outlet for his feelings. Paints provide one such outlet. They help a child to find satisfying expression for his thoughts and desires. They help to open his eyes to wonders. They lead him to explore and experiment. They help strengthen his confidence in the worth of himself and his playmates.

1. Easel Painting

The materials needed for easel painting are brushes, an easel, containers for paint, paper, and smocks.

At first, it is best to limit two-year-olds to one color of

Finger Painting

Easel Painting and Using Clay

Using Puzzles

paint—perhaps red. Later another color may be added. The child likes to make wide movements with his arms. He enjoys seeing the red color appear on the paper. His painting consists only of splashes of color.

The three-year-old begins to experiment with color and form, to make designs and later crude pictures. Two or three bright colors (red, green, yellow) are sufficient for him. If three-year-olds have not painted before, start with one color, perhaps red.

The worker does not suggest to the child what to paint nor ask what he is painting. Avoid such directions as "Do it this way," or "Do it that way." What happens to the child as he works is more important than the finished product. God has placed within each child a desire to create, achieve, and express himself. As he paints, a child is telling with brush and paint how he feels about his world, about God, about those around him. He is gaining confidence in himself if what he puts on paper is accepted by workers.

Three-year-old Steve makes a bold, short stroke with the yellow paint. "This is the sun." He draws a green circle. "This is the snow." He adds a blue arc. "This is the sky." Then, with red he paints a circle around all the forms. "This keeps it all in." Steve is not painting a picture. He is trying to understand the elements of the winter season.

The two- and three-year-old can learn to push the brush against the side of the paint jar and keep it from dripping on the paper or floor. He can learn quickly to paint on the paper—not on his hands, the equipment, or other children. He can also learn that the yellow brush goes back into the yellow paint and not into the red. The worker keeps a wet sponge near for the child to use when the paint drips. A worker avoids making a child feel guilty when he has dripped the paint. She assures him it is all right and suggests that he wipe it up with the sponge. Some of the children will want to take what they have painted home with them; others never mention the paintings again. To dry the paintings, hang them on a clothes rack or the back of a chair.

2. *Finger Painting*

Two-year-olds can usually manage finger painting better than easel painting. It provides an avenue of release to the child who has had no chance for play with mud pies or for messy play at other times. Psychologists tell us that children feel a need for being messy.

The child with hostile feelings finds using finger paints an acceptable way in which to express those feelings. He is finding that there are other ways in which to express the way he feels which are more acceptable than kicking, biting, hitting, or spitting. There is also a feeling of satisfaction and achievement as he moves his hands in the finger paint. "See," he says as he shows what he is doing. After feelings of tension, frustration, and confusion have been released, a child can enjoy richer and happier experiences.

Finger paint may be bought at any art store, or made satisfactorily.

The child stands at a table when using finger paints. The table should be covered with linoleum, Formica, or oilcloth. A plastic apron placed over a smock (man's shirt) protects the child's clothes. About a tablespoon of paint is placed on the surface of the table for the child. He uses his fingers, the palms of his hands, or his wrists. He experiments as he wishes. When he has finished, the worker supervises the washing of his hands, either in the bathroom or in a basin of water nearby. A wet sponge or rag is used to wipe the finger paint when the child has finished.

3. *A Word of Caution*

Some workers like to use coloring books with Nursery children. The books restrain the child's innate creative ability and hinder development. God has placed within each child the ability to create and the urge to develop this ability. Many adults are not able to create because their creativeness was stifled in childhood. Coloring books and mimeographed patterns are harmful not only because the drawings are usually shoddy and lacking in art quality, but also because they demand muscular co-ordination beyond the ability of the child. Trying to keep within the lines may cause tension and frustration.

III. Using Clay

Clay may be bought in moist form ready for use, or in powdered form with directions for moistening. Plastic dough or wallpaper cleaner may be substituted for moist clay. Play dough is inexpensive and easily made from flour, salt, water, and powdered alum. The two- or three-year-old will enjoy the moist clay more because of its texture.

Children first handle the clay by pounding, patting, pinching, and rolling it. Using the clay helps the child to find an acceptable way in which to express and rid himself of unpleasant feelings. He is learning that it is all right to express his feelings, but they must be expressed in an acceptable way rather than by kicking, biting, pinching, or spitting. Again, it is what happens to the child as he uses the clay rather than what he makes that is important. Using the clay helps the child act out his feelings and get rid of hostile feelings. The worker may chant a song as the child pounds, pats, or rolls the clay.

Workers give a child a ball of clay about the size of an orange. He uses it on a plastic-top table or an oilcloth-covered table. His clothes are protected by a smock (man's shirt from which the sleeves and collar have been cut). He enjoys the feel of the clay.

Clay and paints satisfy an emotional need and the experience leads to personality enrichment through what happens inside a child as he uses the materials.

IV. Using Blocks

Blocks furnish another medium through which the little child can express emotions and creative desires and can gain skill in manipulation.

1. *With Toddlers*

The toddler uses Blockbusters, stacking and unstacking them, picking them up, carrying them, putting them down, sitting on them, standing on them, climbing on them and jumping off, laying them end to end, making a road and walking on them. A worker is nearby to give guidance, but the toddler does the building without interference.

As the toddler stacks Blockbusters, a worker may sing a song about stacking the blocks, or she may make the sound of a train, if the blocks have become a train, or she may make just a comment, "I'm glad we have blocks. Jimmie likes blocks."

2. *With Two-Year-Olds*

When a child is first transferred to the Two-Year department, he will enjoy using Blockbusters for a while instead of the wooden educational blocks that are provided for two's. A child may be two years of age chronologically, but a toddler in many other ways. Because of this, Blockbusters will meet his needs at first in the Two-Year department. He will enjoy sitting on them, stepping up and down on them, pushing them, walking on them. He does not build complex forms with blocks. To a child, building with blocks means a manipulating process rather than a definite pattern.

Sometimes the worker sings as the two-year-old works with his blocks. She chants a song that fits in with what the child is doing. Or she may sing about coming to church and the things which we find at church. Sometimes she makes a comment or tells an on-the-spot story about a child and his blocks. She is nearby to give guidance when needed, but allows the child to work with his blocks without interference.

3. *With Three-Year-Olds*

The three-year-old expresses his ideas through the blocks, learns sharing and taking turns. He, too, builds at first without design. During the year, he begins to build with some design. As in other age groups, the worker does not dominate the block activity, but gives guidance when necessary.

4. *Enriching the Child's Experiences*

A child's experiences with blocks may be enriched by on-the-spot stories, songs, or conversation. A worker accepts what the child builds. She does not suggest what to build, nor does she suggest what it could be when he finishes. If he wants to tell her about what he has done, he will do so. A worker should be a good listener.

At times, pictures near the block area will help the child to know how to use the blocks and perhaps suggest some ideas to him. Creativeness with blocks can be further stimulated by adding wooden figures—animals, community helpers, families, or furniture.

V. Using Home-living Materials

Home-living activities provide opportunities for children to grow in appreciation of their parents, to learn to share and take turns, and to develop in appreciation for God's plan for the home and for the things which God helps them to have.

1. *With Toddlers*

A doll, a doll bed, a blanket in which to wrap the doll, and a child-size rocker are sufficient for the toddler. He will rock the doll, wrap the doll in a blanket, put it to bed, and get in the bed himself. As he does so, the worker may

sing an appropriate song, make a comment, use story conversation or a Bible verse. The worker does not expect the
toddler to put away the materials all by himself, but helps
the child in putting away the materials.

2. With Two's and Three's

To the home-living equipment for two's and three's suggested in chapter 3, add a few hats, purses, dress-up clothes,
dust cloths, dishes, and dish cloths. From time to time, add
real fruit and flowers.

Home-living materials provide opportunities for the children to play together, although each child works independently.

Home-living Experiences

3. Experiences

Some of the experiences which may result from the use
of home-living materials are: cooking, serving, and eating
a meal; dressing and undressing, putting to bed, or rocking
the doll; washing and drying the dishes; talking over the
telephones; arranging flowers; playing postman, milkman,

doctor, or groceryman; playing mother and daddy; getting ready for church or shopping; dusting and sweeping; washing and ironing; and dressing up.

Imaginary food is cooked and the children often talk to God before eating the imaginary food. The doll is cared for and a child begins to understand the parent's role. Two children cannot use the rolling pin at the same time. One must wait until the other child has finished. One child cooks the food, another sets the table, while still another cares for the baby. Each has a responsibility. This is the beginning of co-operation as each carries out his responsibility.

A worker avoids entering into the activity unless invited to do so. In watching the child in his activity, the worker may sing, use a story or picture, or make a comment to enrich the experience.

VI. Using Puzzles

Puzzles should be simple and about objects or things with which the child is familiar. They should be wooden with pieces large enough and thick enough for the child to handle easily. A piece of cardboard fitted underneath the movable pieces raises them for easy removal by the child. As the child tries to fit the pieces of a puzzle together he faces the problems of size, color, shape, and the relationship of one piece to another. What is the shape of the piece which fits into a particular place? A puzzle helps a child to think, to solve problems, and to work independently.

VII. Using Nature Materials

Provide materials which children can touch, taste, see, or smell. Bring the outdoors indoors. The toddler will enjoy bright leaves and fresh flowers. Smelling the flowers and hearing the worker say, "God made the flowers," the child begins to form his first concepts of God and the world.

1. *The Worker Interprets*

The attitude, the tone of voice, and facial expression of the worker speak to the child. He joins in wonder and admiration. It is the teacher's reverence and response that the child begins to feel.

If the windows in the room are low enough, the toddler may watch the clouds, birds, rain, stars, or moon; he may feel the warm sunshine on his back. The worker may enrich his experience by singing, making a comment, or using story conversation and Bible verses. The worker will answer each child's questions in words he will understand.

2. *Materials to Use*

Have such nature materials as a bird's nest, cotton bolls, corn in the husk, fruits, vegetables, and large shells for the children to handle and investigate. From these materials will come many questions.

Two- and three-year-olds enjoy watching and caring for goldfish, turtles, and birds. A feeding station for the birds may be made just outside one of the windows in the room. If this is impossible, a worker may go with one or two of the children outside and leave food on the ground. An appreciation of the world begins when the child is very young, if he has had the right kind of experiences with nature.

The nature materials which the child will be likely to find or see in his everyday experiences usually have more teaching value than strange materials from other localities. If a child has an experience of worship as he sees and handles a flower or an animal, he may later have a similar experience with another flower or animal.

SUGGESTED ACTIVITIES

For Workers Who Study This Book

1. Make three columns as follows:

   Materials   Desirable   Undesirable

   In the first column list all of the materials used in your room. In the second and third columns list the desirable or undesirable experiences which the children have had as a result of using the materials during the past month. What can be done to help eliminate the undesirable experiences?

2. Study the following pictures and the others in this chapter to determine what they reveal about the role of the worker in interpreting a child's experiences with materials. Chapter 2 contains many additional pictures which may be used in a similar study.

CHAPTER 7

7

Planning for Good Teaching

NURSERY CHILDREN learn best in a homelike atmosphere in which a flexible program of activities allows each child to participate according to his interests and abilities. Good teaching enables the Nursery child to develop his fullest capacity in religious, emotional, physical, and social growth.

Good teaching requires careful planning. Nursery workers need regular planning meetings to unify the work and maintain the highest standards in procedure. There is need for joint meetings and for organizational meetings.

I. JOINT MEETINGS

At least once a quarter all workers with each Nursery age group (regardless of organization) should meet together to discuss the work which they have in common. For example, all the Sunday school, Training Union, and week-day workers with two-year-olds would meet to discuss their work with two-year-olds. The chairman of the Nursery correlating committee, the director of children's work, or the superintendent or leader of the age group may preside at these meetings. The meeting should include:

DEVOTIONAL TIME: A brief inspirational time creates a spiritual atmosphere.

PRAYER: Pray for personal guidance and for one another.

DISCUSSION OF COMMON PROBLEMS: Plan together regarding such matters as—

(1) *Using and caring for equipment.*—Each worker should accept responsibility.

115

(2) *Guiding children.*—All departments should agree about how directions are to be given and what limits are to be set. It is essential that the guidance used with the children be consistent.

(3) *Selecting materials.*—All workers should be in agreement when new materials are to be purchased and arranged in the room.

(4) *Sharing.*—Information learned about children should be shared, along with experiences the children are having in each group.

(5) *Planning.*—Plan co-operatively for worker activities, such as visitation of each home by all organizations, distribution of *Living with Children,* more effective teaching, and parents' meetings.

II. ORGANIZATIONAL PLANNING MEETINGS

Workers in each organization need to have their own Nursery department meetings in line with the program of the organization. Sunday school Nursery workers meet during the weekly officers and teachers' meeting; Training Union Nursery workers meet during the monthly officers' council. Each organization will hold Nursery planning meetings by departments.

III. PLANNING FOR WORK WITH BABIES OR TODDLERS

Certain basic matters will receive attention in each planning meeting for the Baby department or the Toddler department. Of course the departments will meet separately.

1. Create an atmosphere for the meeting. Help workers to feel the need for daily meditation, prayer, and personal enrichment. Study Bible backgrounds for story conversations which may be used with babies or toddlers. Prayer should permeate the meeting—for guidance in work for each child, for parents, for guidance in finding needed workers.

2. Study basic purposes for Nursery children. Discuss what workers will do to accomplish the basic purposes for

the Nursery age range and the specific purposes of the department.

3. Plan for equipment and materials. Study the present room: Is equipment in the best working arrangement? What should be done to have equipment and materials ready for the next session? Check on such materials as cleansing tissue and disposable diapers. Be sure you have ample supply. List any materials that need to be bought. Delegate responsibility for securing them.

4. Discuss the previous session. What were the weak points? What improvement can be made? What problems arose? How were they handled?

5. Study the children. Have they changed during the past few weeks? In what ways? Are you meeting their needs? Do you have the information you need about each child?

6. Plan for use of materials. Plan ways to use the Bible, pictures, books, record player, songs, and conversation. Learn Nursery songs found in the *Church Nursery Guide*. Encourage workers to share ideas for using material.

7. Plan for visitation. Set a time to visit babies or toddlers who have been absent, prospects for department, and any home where a worker may be helpful. If there are new children in the department, plan to visit the parents to acquaint them with the Nursery program (procedures followed) and how to use *Living with Children*. Look at the articles which would be good for parents of babies or toddlers and the outstanding items in the section for babies or toddlers. Plan a set time for delivering *Living with Children*.

IV. ACTIVITIES FOR WORKERS WITH TWO- AND/OR THREE-YEAR-OLDS

Follow the pattern outlined for workers with babies or toddlers.

1. Create an atmosphere in the devotional period. Discuss

using the Bible for personal enrichment. Consider the Bible story to be used during the next session, studying its background, not for use with the children but for the enrichment of the lives of the workers. Suggest a Bible passage for personal study during the week. Spend some time in prayer.

2. Plan for visitation. Call for reports on contacts with children who have been absent, with analysis of reasons for absence.

Make plans for visitation by the workers who will go into the homes before the beginning of the quarter, taking the magazine *Living with Children* according to the schedule agreed upon. The workers should be prepared to talk with the parents about the particularly appropriate articles and the sections which apply to specific age groups.

3. Discuss teaching plans. Ask workers to share experiences of children in the previous session. Evaluate the department's work. Did equipment and materials meet the needs of the children? How can teaching be improved? Think about the children in the group. What information about each child should workers keep in mind as they make teaching plans? Talk about activities which may result from the use of the present equipment and materials in the room. Decide which workers are to guide a particular activity or activities and which worker will greet the parent at the door and get the child from the group. Learn any Nursery songs which workers do not know.

4. Use a plan sheet. The exact form for the plan sheet will vary according to the organization using it. Begin with a suggested form and adapt it as needed, then follow the pattern agreed upon by the workers for your department. Your plan sheet should provide space for recording information about the following points in respect to each area of activity.

Purpose
Area of Activity
Ways to Use the Bible
Ways to Use Pictures
Bible Verses to Use
Songs and Other Music
Conversation
Bible Stories to Recall
Materials—available and to be secured

5. Prepare for extended session. Plans should be checked in the workers' meeting. Remind the regular workers who are to teach in the extended session. Discuss possible activities; consider problems which may have arisen concerning the extended session. See that the list is ready for parents to sign if the children are remaining.

6. Planning meetings may be used to help workers develop specific skills. From time to time provide for discussion and demonstration of such matters as the following: how to tell stories; how to make up on-the-spot stories; how to talk to the children; how to be a good listener; how to tell a child about a picture; things workers need to know about nature; how to guide a child in talking to God.

V. Suggested Procedures for the Age Groups

Procedures must be flexible if they are to meet the needs of individual Nursery children. Flexibility does not mean a haphazard schedule. Children like routine. For example, the three-year-old likes to know that cleaning up follows activity time; then group time, going to the bathroom, snack time, and resting follow each other in sequence. In the procedure for any Nursery age consider the following steps:

1. As Children Arrive

Plan to have each child greeted by a worker who removes wraps and puts them in the regular place—or guides the child to do it. Babies are settled in their beds.

2. *Activities*

Prepare for activities suited to the experience and maturity of the child. Note the suggested lists given in this chapter.

3. *Group Time*

In the Three-Year department children will come together for group time. The procedure will vary according to the attention and interest of the three-year-olds, using group activities such as—

(1) Talking about a picture; singing a song suggested by the picture; using several Bible verses about the picture; listening to a Bible story; talking to God

(2) Talking about what the children have been doing in activity time; singing a song about these activities; using some Bible verses; playing games; talking to God; listening to the reading of a book

4. *Extended Session*

The constant activity of small children requires that the long session (the Sunday school or the Training Union period plus the preaching service which follows) include many things, such as toileting, washing and drying hands; snack time (fruit juice, milk, or water, and crackers); rest time (10 to 20 minutes), including relaxing and listening to quiet music. There will be activities (chosen by the child) similar to those used in the first activity time, but much briefer. Time should be allowed for unhurried putting away of materials and getting wraps or other belongings.

VI. ACTIVITIES APPROPRIATE FOR VARIOUS AGES

The planning meetings for various Nursery departments will center on providing suitable activities for the children. The following lists will offer helpful guidance.

1. Babies

The child in the Baby department is ready for learning experiences that will begin to develop wholesome attitudes and add to his skills. He—

Plays by himself with toys brought from home or sterilized toys furnished by the church

Listens to quiet music from record player

Plays such games as "peek-a-boo" with worker

Is diapered, fed, bubbled, and cuddled according to schedule

May look at pictures in the Bible

Listens and responds to quiet singing or humming of worker

Responds to worker as she talks to him

Sleeps

Plays in playpen or sits in swing if old enough

2. Toddlers

Toddlers choose activities which allow them to use large body muscles and to experience the pleasure of handling and manipulating things. The toddler will enjoy—

Sitting on doll bed, holding doll, carrying doll, rocking doll

Playing with pushing and pulling toys

Stacking, unstacking, and lining up Blockbusters; walking on Blockbusters; jumping off Blockbusters

Rolling the ball

Hearing music (humming and singing of workers, music from record player)

Playing with washable, cuddly toys

Seeing, feeling, tasting, smelling nature objects, looking out the window

Responding to story conversation

Looking at pictures

Looking at pictures in Bible

Hearing worker talk to God

Looking at books, listening to worker tell about books

Being fed and diapered

Going to bathroom, washing hands

Drinking fruit juice, milk, or water; eating cracker

Resting

3. *Two-Year-Olds*

The two-year-old has progressed to the stage where activity areas are more meaningful. We find him making his own choice and—

Enjoying the home-living area—rocking the doll, taking care of the doll, putting doll to bed, making things to eat, washing the dishes, stacking and unstacking the dishes, dusting, talking on telephone, putting dishes on the table, eating imaginary food

Building with blocks—stacking and unstacking, pushing, lining up blocks for roads and bridges, making fences, putting animals inside

Enjoying nature materials—caring for growing things; handling nature objects; tasting foods, such as fruits and vegetables; experimenting with seeds; looking out the window

Hearing worker talk to God; talking to God

Looking at books—turning pages independently, listening to worker read book

Looking at pictures—playing a picture game, talking with worker about picture, imitating children in picture

Working puzzles

Painting at the easel

Using clay—pounding, pinching, rolling, squeezing

Enjoying music—listening to records

Other activities—talking with worker, listening to story, hearing worker sing, using the Bible, putting away materials

4. *Three-Year-Olds*

Three's will enjoy many of the activities listed for the two's, but there will be more purposefulness and more willingness to do things together. For example, in the home-living area, three's will enjoy such activities as cooking, caring for the baby, washing and drying dishes, dusting, talking on the telephone, dressing like Mother, setting the table, using dough to make food, eating imaginary meals, cleaning house, and going to the store. These activities initiated by the child provide opportunities for him to make his own decisions; develop his imagination and initiative; do his own thinking, planning, and following through; solve his own problems; accept responsibility; and find natural ways to get along with people.

There will be similar evidences of maturity in the three-year-old's activities in other areas.

SUGGESTED ACTIVITIES

For Workers Who Study This Book

1. Briefly list in order what happened at your last planning meeting. Compare it with the suggested procedures found in this chapter. How can the planning meeting be made more helpful to your Nursery workers?
2. Plan to improve your present procedure. List in one column the procedures followed in your department. List in a parallel column the procedures which should be followed in your department. Compare the two columns. Consider how your present procedure can be improved.

CHAPTER 8

I. VISITATION

    1. The Purpose
    2. Accomplishing the Purpose

II. PARENT MEETINGS

    1. Intra-organizational Meetings
    2. Workshops
    3. Meetings Based on Films or Filmstrips
    4. Question Periods
    5. Lecture Periods
    6. The Orientation Meeting
    7. Panels
    8. Other Types of Parent Meetings
    9. Caring for the Children

III. OTHER WAYS OF WORKING WITH THE HOME

    1. Using Parents in Extended Session
    2. Providing Information

8

Working with the Home

THE MOST influential factor in the religious growth of a child is his home. The guidance which he receives at church strengthens that which he receives at home. The church and the home must each know what the other is trying to do for the child. Church-home relationship is a two-way process.

There is no one way in which such a relationship may be brought about. It is the result of frequent and purposeful contacts between church and parents in home visitations, in conferences at church, in parent meetings, and in social hours together.

I. VISITATION

The attitude of the worker who visits is most important. A worker should visit from a deep, genuine interest in the child. It is necessary to understand the child and his home environment in order to help him grow. An improved understanding of the child comes from seeing him in his everyday living.

A worker who visits makes new friends, deepens friendships, and serves others. When visiting in the interest of the child, the worker is received as a friend by parents and child.

Visitation should help parents understand the purposes of the Nursery department and how they are accomplished. The visitor clarifies for the parents the ways in which children are taught at church. "I bring my child to church to learn about God, and not to play," says one parent. The worker can help this parent to understand that one of the most important ways in which a child learns is through play. A child's play is not something to take up his time. It is his work.

A worker visits when a child is absent. John had been absent from Sunday school many Sundays. No one in the Three-Year department had visited him. Finally, a worker who had been assigned John decided to go and see him. She went to the home but no one answered the doorbell. She was about to leave when a neighbor called, "Did you want to see someone at the Anderson's?"

"Yes," replied the worker.

"They aren't at home," said the neighbor, "John is in the hospital seriously ill. The Andersons spend all their time at the hospital."

What an opportunity this worker and her department had missed to be of service in a time of need.

Spiritual preparation is essential for effective visitation. No visit should be made until the worker has first talked to God and asked his guidance. The relationship with God helps the worker to feel more secure about the outcome of the visit.

1. *The Purpose*

The purpose of visitation in the Nursery departments is twofold: a ministry to the child and a ministry to the parents.

Ministry to the child includes winning his friendship and confidence and assuring him of the visitor's interest in him as an individual; understanding better the child's special interests, his home environment, and his reaction to Nursery workers; helping the child feel that the Nursery worker is his special friend; showing interest in a child through remembering his birthday and other occasions; and encouraging his regular attendance.

Some workers have found that the most effective visitation with the child can be made when the worker takes the child a mounted magazine picture, a pretty flower, a growing plant (sweet potato or carrot top in water), or a sprouted bean to place in a glass of dirt. In the visit the child and his parents will enjoy hearing Nursery songs and short stories.

Ministry to the parents includes winning the lost parents to Christ and encouraging unaffiliated Baptists to join the church; encouraging the establishment and strengthening of family worship; helping parents to understand how regular attendance benefits the child; interpreting to the parents *Living with Children* and the work of the department; and enlisting parents in Sunday school and Training Union.

2. Accomplishing the Purpose

The superintendent or leader is responsible for seeing that effective visitation is done.

(1) *Engage in regular visitation.*—Both the Sunday school and the Training Union depend on regular visitation for a major part of their ministry to the home.

The Sunday school Nursery department enrolment is divided into groups (often arranged geographically). Each group will be assigned to a worker for the entire Sunday school year, unless a child is transferred out of the department. Helpful information gleaned from visitation will be shared at the officers and teachers' meeting.

In Training Union, definite assignments are not stabilized for the whole year but are made to workers by the department leaders on a weekly, monthly, or quarterly basis, depending on the purpose of visitation. The children may be assigned to different workers for each visitation.

The department superintendent or the leader may find it advisable to make tactful changes in assignments when it is felt that a worker other than the one assigned might better meet the needs of the home. Reassignment may be needed because the group becomes too large for one worker, because there have been personality clashes, or when there is continued negative response on the part of the home.

Usually the department superintendent or leader does not take a group to visit regularly but will visit every home at least once during the year. She should assist the other workers when transportation is needed and when the worker is prevented from visiting because of illness or other reasons.

(2) *Use special visitation.*—Because it is important for every worker to know every child and for every child to feel that every worker is interested in him, it is advisable for each worker to accept the responsibility of visiting children other than her own group two or three times during the year—in addition to her regular visitation. This special visitation will be done at a time decided upon by the department. One week of the second month of each quarter would be desirable.

These special assignments will be made at the Sunday school weekly officers and teachers' meeting and the Training Union monthly officers' council. Testimonies and reports are shared at the next planning meeting. If the church has a weekly visitation program and the department has a meeting for assignments and reports, the superintendent or leader will make the assignments then.

(3) *Promote prospect visitation.*—Every worker in the department should be alert for prospects. The superintendent or leader may assign the prospects. When a child who has not been visited previously joins the Sunday school or Training Union, the superintendent or leader may visit in that home during the following week. The newly enrolled child should then be assigned to a group for regular visitation during the remainder of the church year.

II. PARENT MEETINGS

The most common means for parents and workers to communicate with each other is through a parent meeting. These meetings are useful only when they serve a distinct purpose which is of mutual concern to both parents and workers and when parents and workers participate.

1. *Intra-organizational Meetings*

It is wise to plan some meetings with all organizations participating. For example, all of the parents of and workers with children three years old in Sunday school, Training Union, and on weekdays will come together for a meeting. The Nursery correlating committee will be responsible for the combined meetings. It is wise to schedule the meetings in time to have them included in the church calendar. Parents can then set up their schedules well in advance.

Additional Nursery meetings may be planned to meet special needs. There will be times when the meetings will include parents of all Nursery children, regardless of age. At other times, the meeting will be for a specific department. The meetings should be publicized well in advance by use of the church bulletin, posters, handbills, and the newspaper.

Some churches feel that a combined meeting each quarter is helpful. This plan gives an opportunity for parents to get together with workers at least four times a year. There may be situations in which it will be impossible to have four meetings a year. In any situation there should be at least one combined meeting each year.

The leader is the key to a successful parent meeting. This person needs to be one who can lead discussions, who knows how to draw people out, who enjoys leading a conference, and knows how to start and stop a meeting.

The length of the meeting is important. One hour is usually sufficient. It is better to dismiss when interest is high.

2. *Workshops*

Parents as well as children enjoy making something. Watch the joy Daddy gets from making a piece of equipment for a Nursery department. Parents like "to help fix things for my child's room." Daddies can make pieces of equipment from apple boxes and orange crates, while mothers sew doll clothes and bed linens, mend sheets, and do many other things. Old equipment may be refinished and made more attractive. Pictures can be cut out of magazines and catalogs and mounted. The list of what parents can do is unlimited.

One church that did not have money to pay for the painting of Nursery rooms bought paint and invited parents to a painting party. The result was clean, attractive rooms for the Nursery children and fellowship and fun for the parents.

3. *Meetings Based on Films or Filmstrips*

Keep in mind that showing films is not for entertainment but to provide a springboard for discussion. Films should tie in with what has gone on before. The parents may find the answers to their questions, or emphasis may be placed on the Christian home.

First Steps in Religion is an excellent filmstrip to tie in with Christian Home Week. The film shows the place of a family in helping a child to form his concept of God and Christian living.

There should be some preparation for the film or filmstrip before it is shown. The leader may prepare questions for the parents to answer from seeing the film or divide the parents into groups to look for a specific thing in the film.

For example, *Terrible Twos and Trusting Threes* (20 min.) is an excellent film on the characteristics of two- and three-year-olds. The parents may be divided into two groups. One group may write down all the words they hear in the film which tell what the two-year-old is like. The other group may write down all the words they hear which tell what the three-year-old is like. At the close of the film, the leader may guide a discussion on what each has found.

Many public libraries and state universities have free

films available. State and county health departments lend free of charge films on child development. Films may be rented from your Baptist Book Store or from the New York University Film Library, New York City, New York.

The following films may be used: *Preface to Life, Life with Baby, Baby Meets Parents, Children Learn by Experience, As the Twig Is Bent,* and *Answering the Child's Why.* Additional films may be found in *Focus,* the catalog published by the Audio-Visual Aids Department of the Baptist Sunday School Board.

A film should always be previewed by the leader before it is shown.

4. Question Periods

From time to time parents ask Nursery workers questions. Often this is done when they bring the child to church, and the Nursery worker does not have adequate time to answer fully. A time could be planned when parents and workers get together for discussing their questions.

The leader who says, "Now, do you have any questions?" will be met only by blank stares. Some parents will hesitate to ask their questions in a group. Therefore, the wise leader will prepare a list of eight or ten questions which can be typed or mimeographed and given out at the beginning of the meeting. The parents may choose the question which they want answered. Soon parents will be asking questions of their own. Do not prolong the meeting.

5. Lecture Periods

There are times when it is good to have a specialist address the parent-worker meeting. A doctor may talk about the physical development of the child; a person from the health department, about nutrition; a pastor or someone else, on the spiritual development of the child; or an authority on child development, on what to expect of the child at certain stages of development. It is important that the person selected to lecture be an authority in his field and know how to talk to people. The lecture may be followed by questions and discussion. Certainly, lecture meetings should be used sparingly.

6. *The Orientation Meeting*

This type of meeting is usually held before children are transferred to another department. The parents come to the room where the child will be assigned, and actually use the materials which their child will be using. They do not act childish or even pretend to be children. They use the materials to see how the child has learning experiences with them. They may learn some songs which the children will be singing. Someone will present the purposes for the department, lead the parents in understanding why certain materials are used with this age group, and show how the child can have learning experiences which will help him to develop to his fullest capacity. At this meeting, parents and workers can find what each group expects of the other.

7. *Panels*

The reading panel is a helpful feature for a meeting. The parents go to books to find their information and bring to the parent group a report of what they have found. For example, parents are asking about behavior problems of the two-year-old. This becomes the core of their reading and they report to the group what they have read and, in the discussion which follows, try to come up with some answers.

Another type of panel is an informal discussion by certain members of the parent group. From four to six parents may be asked to serve on the panel. They do not have set speeches, but say what they feel as the discussion moves along. Suppose a parent group wants to discuss discipline.

A mother, a pastor, a psychologist, a nursery school teacher, and a father may be asked to serve on the panel. The leader introduces the subject and the discussion begins. It is up to the leader to keep the panel going.

8. *Other Types of Parent Meetings*

Parent-worker meetings should be varied. No parent wants to hear the same thing every time he comes to a meeting. He wants to find something that will meet his own particular need.

Parents need to know one another. Sometimes the parent meeting will take the form of open house, tea party, or outing. Such occasions help the parents to become acquainted with one another and with the workers.

9. *Caring for the Children*

In some churches a Young People's department is asked to co-operate with the Nursery workers in planning for the children during the parent meeting. The young people go into the homes to be with the children during the hour the parents are in the meeting.

Other churches provide a teaching program for the children of the church, just as they would on Sunday morning or on Sunday night. Those in charge are people who know how to provide good learning experiences for the children and who have previously met with the Nursery workers to plan what will be done when the children are in the Nursery departments during the workers' meeting. The *Church Nursery Guide* is designed for use by workers who have the children during the week or on Sunday. Nursery units are available for use when a church has a week of training.

III. OTHER WAYS OF WORKING WITH THE HOME

In addition to visitation and parents' meetings, there are a number of ways in which the home-church relationship can be strengthened and made increasingly vital.

1. *Using Parents in the Extended Session*

Parents may assist the Nursery workers during the extended sessions, but not in the room where their child is. Other church members may participate in this service. All workers for the extended session should be encouraged to study *Church Nursery Guide* and attend the planning meetings preceding the sessions they are to teach.

2. *Providing Information*

Use a bulletin board placed in the entrance hall for attractive displays of helpful information. This may include articles clipped from magazines or newspapers, suggested books and leaflets for reading, and other information which will prove helpful to parents.

County or city health departments are glad to supply workers with leaflets on child development. Make these available to the parents. Some insurance companies make available free of charge excellent leaflets on child development.

In one church a Nursery worker keeps a supply of free leaflets from the health department. Parents have learned to look forward to receiving the leaflets.

Other leaflets which may be distributed are "The Art of Religious Conversation in the Home," and "How Your Child Learns about God." These may be purchased from the Baptist Book Store.

When books on child development are available through the church library or the public library, inform the parents by card, letter, or notice on the bulletin board.

Some Nursery workers and parents work together on a monthly or quarterly bulletin which goes to Nursery parents, the pastor, Training Union director, Sunday school superintendent, deacons, and members of the Nursery correlating committee. Instead of making the bulletin a newssheet, various topics of interest to parents are discussed, such as the selection of toys and books, parent-child relationship, and various aspects of a child's life.

Working together, parents and Nursery workers find satisfaction in knowing that they are trying to do their best for the person who is central in all our ministries, THE CHILD.

SUGGESTED ACTIVITIES

For Workers Who Study This Book

1. Assume that regular meetings of the parents of Nursery children are desirable in your church.
   (1) Write down the needs of the parents which you feel should be met in these meetings.
   (2) List at least three different types of meetings which you think would meet these needs.
2. Choose one of the meetings you have suggested.
   (1) Write out in detail the preparations necessary for the kind of meeting you have chosen. Include the committees, publicity, and the delegation of responsibilities.
   (2) Write out in detail what should take place in the meeting.
3. Study the following picture and point out what it reveals about (1) carry-over from home-living experiences the child has had at church, and (2) the importance of acquainting parents with the teaching methods used in the Nursery department.

CHAPTER 9

I. LITERATURE

    1. Periodical for the Workers
    2. Periodicals for Parents
    3. Teaching Pictures

II. FILMSTRIPS

III. STANDARD OF EXCELLENCE

IV. PREVIEW STUDY

V. RESOURCE MATERIALS

    1. Free Helps
    2. Books for Workers and Parents
    3. Sources of Helpful Pamphlets for Parents and Workers
    4. Sources of Catalogs for Equipment and Supplies

9

Helps for Effective Work

PROVIDING the right kind of learning experiences for Nursery children requires more than wishful thinking. There must be careful planning and trained workers who take advantage of all helps available.

I. LITERATURE

The same Nursery curriculum materials are for use by the Sunday school and the Training Union, and by all persons who are in charge of children in the Nursery room at any time during the week. The experiences that a child has at any time in a Nursery room should contribute toward the objectives discussed in chapter 5.

1. *Periodical for the Workers*

Church Nursery Guide is a quarterly periodical for workers who teach in Nursery departments of the church. It offers plans for use on Sunday morning, Sunday evening, or in any session during the week. Each issue contains suggestions for equipment and materials, recommended procedures, songs, stories, and other helpful information. The use of this periodical by all workers who are with Nursery children at the church at any time will help to assure unity in methods, materials, and purposes and to make possible happy, enriching experiences every time a child comes to church.

Church Nursery Guide is published quarterly by the Baptist Sunday School Board. It should be ordered at the same time the literature for all organizations is ordered.

2. *Periodicals for Parents*

The quarterly periodical for parents of Nursery children is *Living with Children*. Each issue contains articles of special interest to parents, suggested home activities, stories, and songs. The periodical helps parents to become acquainted with the activities of the Nursery departments of the church.

Nursery workers should see that this periodical gets into every home every quarter. In families having more than one Nursery child, the department having the oldest child is responsible for delivering *Living with Children* to the parents. It will be necessary to check the enrolment of all Nursery departments in Sunday school and Training Union to learn which department has this responsibility.

The name of the parents should be written on the periodical. It should be carried into the home before the first day of the new quarter. If this is impossible, it should be given to the parents at church on the last Sunday of the quarter. When the latter plan is followed, the periodical should be given on Sunday morning to all parents whose children are present in a Nursery department. If there are parents who are absent on Sunday morning and whose children are enrolled in Training Union, their periodical should be given them that night or during the following week, by the Training Union workers. For the other children enrolled in the Sunday school whose parents were not present the last Sunday morning of the quarter, this periodical should be delivered to their parents during the following week by the Sunday school workers.

Each worker with Nursery children at church should read *Living with Children* regularly. This is necessary preparation in order to call the parents' attention to items of special interest. The worker also learns how the church and the home can complement each other.

There are several reasons for giving the parent a periodical rather than giving the child a leaflet.

(1) Nursery children many times lose, chew, wrinkle, or dirty the leaflet, making it impossible for the parent to use.

(2) The absent child seldom gets a leaflet. Often workers forget to give the children the leaflets, since they leave at different times.

(3) Giving out the leaflets at the door can cause confusion.

(4) More material can be placed in a periodical.

(5) The periodical provides an incentive for visitation and personal conferences.

(6) Sometimes parents have several children within the Nursery age group. The periodical combines material for all ages and makes it easier for the parent to use.

Home Life is a magazine published monthly for use in the home. It is designed for each member of the family with stories, special articles, suggestions for daily family worship, and other interesting features.

3. *Teaching Pictures*

Church Nursery Pictures are published in a set of twenty carefully selected pictures, available from the Baptist Sunday School Board. Each department should have at least one set of the pictures. Since they may be used over and over, they should be given proper care.

II. FILMSTRIPS

Two color filmstrips on Nursery work have been produced by the Baptist Sunday School Board, and may be purchased in Baptist Book Stores.

Providing for Nursery Children (39 frames) is for use by workers with Nursery children, the Nursery correlating committee, and other church planning committees. It shows the purposes of Nursery work, needs of Nursery children, organization, and desired outcomes of Nursery work.

Guiding Nursery Children (32 frames) is designed to help workers to provide proper learning experiences for Nursery children. It contains suggestions about literature and other guidance materials.

III. STANDARD OF EXCELLENCE

The contractor constructing a building follows a blueprint. The housewife baking a cake follows a recipe. The mathematician solving a problem uses a formula. Nursery workers need a blueprint, recipe, or formula for Nursery work. This is found in the Standard of Excellence. The Standard is a balanced program of work for a department. It reveals weak points in the work and is the basis for continuous progress.

In the regular planning meetings of the respective organizations, Nursery workers should use the Nursery Standard for their organization to measure their work to learn which points have been attained and to make plans for attaining the other points.

IV. PREVIEW STUDY

The "Nursery Preview Study" leaflet is designed to help Nursery workers become better teachers through a study of the curriculum materials, study helps, and teaching aids before a quarter begins. This preview enables workers to make long-range plans for their work.

Credit in the Church Study Course for Teaching and Training may be received for the preview study, provided the regular requirements as set forth in the leaflet have been met.

V. RESOURCE MATERIALS

Many workers are constantly looking for additional helps for improving themselves. The materials suggested below can provide this kind of help.

1. *Free Helps*

Free materials on Nursery work are available from your state Sunday school or Training Union department, from the superintendent of Nursery Work in the Sunday School Department, or from the director of Nursery Work in the Training Union Department of the Baptist Sunday School Board, Nashville, Tennessee.

2. *Books for Workers and Parents*

Workers and parents need to understand the Nursery age child. Books such as the following can give new insights into child life. Even though these books may contain some things we cannot endorse, they will furnish many good ideas.

Black, Irma Simonton. *Off to a Good Start.* New York: Harcourt, Brace and Company, 1946

Hurlock, Elizabeth B. *Child Development.* New York: McGraw-Hill Book Company, Inc., 1956

Hymes, James L., Jr. *Understanding Your Child.* Englewood Cliffs, N.J.: Prentice-Hall, 1952

Hymes, James L., Jr. *A Child Development Point of View.* Englewood Cliffs, N.J.: Prentice-Hall, 1956

Frances Ilg and Louise Bates Ames. *Child Behavior.* New York: Harper and Brothers, 1955

Jenkins, Gladys, Helen Schacter, and William W. Bauer. *These Are Your Children.* Chicago: Scott, Foresman and Company, 1953 (Expanding edition)

Ward, Muriel. *Young Minds Need Something to Grow On.* Evanston: Row, Peterson and Company, 1957

Read, Katherine H. *The Nursery School.* Philadelphia: W. B. Sauders Company, 1955

Rudolph, Marguerita. *Living and Learning in Nursery School.* New York: Harper and Brothers, 1954

Spock, Benjamin M. *Common Sense of Baby and Child Care.* New York: Duell, Sloan and Pearch, Inc., 1946

Strang, Ruth. *An Introduction to Child Study.* New York: The Macmillan Company, 1951

Whitehouse, Elizabeth S. *The Children We Teach.* Philadelphia: The Judson Press, 1950

3. *Sources of Helpful Pamphlets for Parents and Workers*

Pamphlets usually contain the latest suggestions or viewpoints on a subject. The cost per copy is usually only a few cents. Nursery workers will find many helpful suggestions in pamphlets from nonreligious organizations such as the following. The Baptist Sunday School Board does not necessarily endorse all that these pamphlets contain.

The Child Study Association of America
132 East 74th Street, New York 21, New York

National Association for Mental Health, Inc.
1790 Broadway, New York 19, New York

National Association for Nursery Education
430 Michigan Avenue, Chicago 5, Illinois

The New York State Society for Mental Health
State Charities Aid Association
105 East 22nd Street, New York 10, New York

The National Society for Crippled Children and Adults
11 South LaSalle Street, Chicago 3, Illinois

Public Affairs Pamphlets
22 East 38th Street, New York 16, New York

Science Research Association
57 West Grand Avenue, Chicago 10, Illinois

Sixty-Nine Bank Street Publications
69 Bank Street, New York 14, New York

Teachers' College, Columbia University
Bureau of Publications, New York 27, New York

United States Office of Education Bulletins
Superintendent of Documents
Government Printing Office, Washington 25, D. C.

4. *Sources of Catalogs for Equipment and Supplies*

Catalogs are vital for information. Equipment and supplies are constantly being improved. Current catalogs show the latest equipment available and usually indicate the ages for which it is designed. However, many companies sell only through local stores. Request catalogs from the following sources:

Baptist Book Store

Childcraft Equipment Company, Inc.
155 East 23rd Street, New York 10, New York

Community Playthings
Rifton, New York

Creative Playthings, Inc.
5 University Place, New York 3, New York

Holgate Brothers Company
Kane, Pennsylvania

The Judy Company
310 North Second Street, Minneapolis, Minnesota

National Dairy Council
111 North Canal Street, Chicago, Illinois

Novo Educational Toy and Equipment Center, Inc.
201 Eighth Avenue, New York 11, New York

Playskool Manufacturing Company
1750 North Lawndale Avenue, Chicago, Illinois

Sifo Company
353 Rosable Street, St. Paul 1, Minnesota

Southern Desk Company
Hickory, North Carolina

SUGGESTED ACTIVITIES

For Workers Who Study This Book

1. List all the helps for effective work mentioned in this chapter.
2. Put an x by the ones you have and have used.
3. Make a list of those which you do not have, but would like to secure.
4. Give the list to the person responsible for obtaining materials for your group.

QUESTIONS FOR REVIEW AND EXAMINATION

CHAPTER 1

1. Why are the early years of childhood important?
2. In what ways do workers influence the early life of a child?
3. What are your particular responsibilities in the group in which you teach?
4. In what ways can a Nursery correlating committee help to improve the Nursery work of a church?

CHAPTER 2

5. Think of two children in the age group which you teach, or two Nursery children you know. In what ways do they differ? How are they alike?
6. List briefly the things that a worker should know about a Nursery child.
7. What way or ways have you found most effective in getting to know the children whom you teach?

CHAPTER 3

8. Rate your present room as to the following by putting excellent, good, and fair after each word: space, location, type of floor, lighting, heating, walls, and toilet facilities.
9. How can your present facilities be improved?
10. Name four principles to keep in mind in arranging equipment and materials in a room.

CHAPTER 4

11. List the equipment which you now use in your room. Draw a line through the equipment which should be discarded. List the additional equipment which you would like to use in your room.
12. In what ways can your room arrangement be improved?
13. What can you do to help improve the Nursery situation in your church?

CHAPTER 5

14. What are the Nursery teaching objectives?
15. In what ways can these objectives be accomplished?
16. Suggest one way to use the Bible, pictures, books, and music in achieving one of these objectives.

CHAPTER 6

17. Name at least one value of each of these materials: stories, paints, clay, blocks, home-living materials, puzzles, and nature.
18. How do the above mentioned materials relate to the Nursery teaching objectives?

CHAPTER 7

19. What three factors are found in every planning meeting?
20. What are the values of a planning meeting?
21. Describe briefly the last session in which you taught.

CHAPTER 8

22. List some ways of working with the home.
23. List at least four ways which you think would be effective in working with the Nursery parents in your church.
24. How may parents be used in the extended session?
25. Describe briefly two types of parent meetings.

CHAPTER 9

26. What are some helps for more effective work?
27. List at least three books which you have read within the last year which have helped you, or three books you plan to read to help you become a better Nursery worker.
28. List three you would like to read during the next year.